THE WISDOM OF THE FOREST

THE AUTHOR

Geoffrey Parrinder is Professor of the Comparative Study of Religions in the University of London. After ordination he spent twenty years teaching in West Africa and studying African religions, and became the founder member of the Department of Religious Studies in the University College of Ibadan, Nigeria. He has travelled widely in Africa, and in India, Pakistan, Ceylon, Burma, Iran, Israel, Jordan and Turkey and held lecturing appointments in Australia, America and India, and at Oxford. He is the author of many books on world religions which have been translated into eight languages.

THE WISDOM
OF THE FOREST

Selections from the Hindu Upanishads

TRANSLATED
BY GEOFFREY PARRINDER

A NEW DIRECTIONS BOOK

Manufactured in the United States of America
First published clothbound and as New Directions Paperbook 414 in 1976
by arrangement with Sheldon Press, London

Library of Congress Cataloging in Publication Data

Upanishads. English. Selections.
  The wisdom of the forest.

  (A New Directions Book)
   A companion volume to Thomas Merton's The wisdom
  of the desert and Irmgard Schloegl's The
  wisdom of the Zen masters.
   I. Parrinder, Edward Geoffrey. II. Title.
BL1120.A3P35 1976   294.5'921   75-42114
ISBN 0-8112-0606-8
ISBN 0-8112-0607-6 pbk.

New Directions Books are published for James Laughlin
by New Directions Publishing Corporation,
333 Sixth Avenue, New York 10014

THE WISDOM OF THE FOREST

IN the forests and quiet places of India many thoughtful men and women have meditated upon truth and sought for union with the universal being. They were not satisfied with possessions or comfort, 'Can wealth bring immortality?' they asked. Their desire for knowledge was a quest for that wisdom which enlightens the present and shows man his eternal role. In the first millennium B.C. there was a great development of this search, though it had begun long before and has continued ever since. The teachings of these sages, for long recorded and passed on by memory, provide some of the greatest treasures that India offers to mankind.

The word 'forest' was used in a wide and general manner, for any piece of uncultivated land could be so called even if it was not thickly wooded. Some ascetics did go into the depths of the jungle or scaled forbidding mountains. There they suffered tortures from heat and cold, rain and wind, wild animals and insects, hunger and thirst. In this deep forest also might be supposed to dwell dangerous forces, gods, and demons, awareness of whom was taken for granted by ascetics who tried to master all powers and transcend the universe.

Other sages lived near villages and towns, where the ideal was to meditate underneath a tree, by a river, alone or attended by a wife or students, and as a Buddhist text says, 'with a village nearby for support'.

There were those here also who practised harsh self-denial, standing up for long periods, holding arms in the air or gazing at the sun. In later times, and no doubt earlier, some of these ascetics were not always reputable and by lying on beds of spikes or sitting by blazing fires in the sun they would torture themselves in order to gain the admiration of less athletic by-standers.

Many of the more thoughtful and earnest forest sages, however, were less rigorous in methods of self-discipline and were simple seekers after wisdom. Some of them lived alone near towns and others were in communities under the guidance of teachers (*gurus*). Hermitages (*ashrams*) were quiet places where people retired for thought and study, and life there was an idyll. Other sages travelled about, singly or in groups, teaching pupils or engaging in debates with other scholars. Extreme ascetics wore few or no clothes, but most of them had simple garments which were needed for protection against the weather.

A forest-dwelling 'stage of life' (also called an *ashram*) was traditional as a retirement at the end of active life. The Laws of Manu, composed about this period, give these directions: 'When a householder sees his skin wrinkled and his hair white, and sees the birth of his grandsons, then he may resort to the forest . . . either committing his wife to his sons or accompanied by her.'

Indian religion has often been termed 'world-denial', but for the ordinary person there were three, later four, stages of life through which he should normally pass. The first stage was that of a student when a young man would receive traditional education. Then came the longest stage, that of the householder who would marry and produce children, and only when his grandsons appeared, to ensure the family line and ancestral rituals, would he pass to the next stage. The forest-dweller (*vana-prastha*), as we have seen, could live with or without his wife. The married ascetic was quite common, since the law books speak of the relationships of the couple, both of whom would be getting on in years. Quiet meditation and preparation for death was the purpose of this final stage of retreat, as in other cultures men retire with a pension or a golden handshake to watch television or play golf.

A fourth stage, that of a complete ascetic (*sannyasi*) may have developed as a more energetic form of austerity, when the wife was left altogether. Then the ascetic might retreat to the deep forest or high mountain for severe exercises, or wander away as a beggar to a holy place, especially to great pilgrimage centres like Benares, where he would await death.

The location of these forests was northern India and later the south comes into view, though no doubt it had a previous history of holy men. Early city cultures had flourished in the plains of the Indus river and its tributaries in north-western India, beyond modern Delhi. These first cities were destroyed chiefly by invading Aryan tribes from central Asia during the second millennium B.C. In time the Aryan and other populations mingled, settled down and moved eastwards into the plains of the river Ganges. There are not many geographical indications in our book, but we read of rivers that flow east and west, like the Indus and the Ganges, and of Benares on the middle Ganges and Videha farther east.

Destruction of the cities of the Indus plains left a long gap in Indian architectural remains, but from the middle of the first millennium B.C. towns and cities can be traced in the Ganges valley. In the sixth or fifth centuries B.C. there lived in this region Mahavira, one of the greatest ascetic teachers of the Jain religion, succeeded shortly after by the more moderate asceticism of Gautama the Buddha. They were associated with Rajagaha or Rajgir, in Bihar, a city whose defences were twenty-five miles long and of which some traces remain today. Other towns flourished before this time and it was clearly a period of prosperity and expansion. Leisure was possible, both to discuss religious and philosophical problems and to support those holy men whose presence was thought to bring blessing to their neighbourhood. There was a great deal of coming and going between town and country. King Janaka, one of the most inquiring and generous monarchs, invited many sages to his court at Videha for the philosophical tournaments in which he delighted, and it must be supposed that these scholars came from a variety of places, forest and city.

The first religious texts of India are the Vedas, for unfortunately the forms of writing that appear in the ruins of the Indus Valley culture have not yet been deciphered. The word Veda means 'knowledge', being related to the English word 'wit'. These Vedic hymns are divine knowledge, songs chanted by priests in favour of the gods of the Aryan invaders, though among some incomprehensible passages there are also the beginnings of speculation about the unity of the divine being, the origins of the universe and life after death. The Vedas are principally concerned with sacrifice and ritual, with sacred words which had a power of their own, and with the importance of the priesthood. The texts were learnt by heart, preserved by great feats of memory, and not committed to writing for many centuries. This process made their use very repetitive and emphasized the power of the spoken word or spell.

The Vedas were succeeded by the Brahmanas, lengthy texts for the Brahmin priests and very tedious to a modern reader. These in turn were followed by the Aranyakas, 'forest treatises' and the Upanishads, 'sessions'. These are all formally part of the Vedic literature, though the Upanishads are sometimes called Vedanta, 'Veda's end'. Countless other compositions followed, often composed orally but written down with less reserve than the early Vedas. Indian literature is vast: epic, legend, ritual, theology, philosophy, ethics, law, poetry, drama, and so on, but it is with the Upanishads that we are concerned here.

The Upanishads, 'sessions' from roots meaning 'sit down near', are the real source of much of the philosophy of Hinduism. The Aranyakas are still concerned with sacrifice, and so to some extent are the early Upanishads though they move away to speculation and discussion between sages. As has been well said,

'The dry bones of the Vedic ritual cult frequently rattle about in them in quite a noisy fashion, and seriously strain our patience and our charity'. But 'the Upanishads are the earliest Hindu treatises, other than single hymns or brief passages, which deal with philosophic subjects'.[1] The Upanishads are the product of the sages of forest and town, and they explore the problems of the divine and human being in ways that have influenced Indian thought ever since.

Critical scholars date the first Upanishads about 600 B.C., though some Indian writers put them much earlier. It was the beginning of that Golden Age of religious and philosophical development that has often been remarked as spreading right across the civilized world. It was the time of Jeremiah, after the first but before the second Isaiah. Pythagoras was shortly to flourish in Greece while Socrates, Plato and Aristotle came later. Zoroaster lived in Persia about this time and Confucius in China. The Buddha and Mahavira lived in India and the Taoists were soon to flourish in China. Intellectual development, and some economic stability, no doubt favoured the growth of philosophical schools, with students attached to a teacher or going from one to another with inquiries.

The Upanishads are of crucial and lasting importance but they are far from easy reading. They open with a passage, not quoted here, wherein the Vedic bones rattle as it tries to identify the sacrifice of a horse with the various parts of the universe. They proceed to speculations on the origins of the world and not

1. F. Edgerton, *The Beginnings of Indian Philosophy*, 1965, p. 28.

infrequently they contain passages that are virtually untranslatable. It is a common fallacy that religious books are easy, for even the apparently simple Gospels profess to contain secret teachings. The Upanishads are much more difficult but happily they contain narratives as well as discourses and these light up the reader's way. Many sages are named and details of their lives and characters appear alongside their teachings. There is also a great deal of repetition, for as teachers they knew its value, and this was preserved in transmitting these doctrines down the ages. Most passages in the early Upanishads are in prose, after the verse of the early Vedas, but soon they return to verse since such forms are better memorized. Verse is also more enigmatic and this resembled the divine utterances, for it was wryly remarked that 'the gods love the cryptic and dislike the obvious'.

The sages of the Upanishads were mostly, though not all, of the Brahmin priestly class. This does not mean that they were active priests engaged in sacrifice and there is growing criticism of rigid adherence to ritual. The word Brahmin in these texts usually simply indicates a scholar or sage. It may seem surprising that some of the questioners of these sages were women, but women also of course belonged to the Brahmin class and some were interested in philosophy. Other teachers, however, belonged to the ruler and warrior class and there are fascinating problems in their traditions and relationships with the priests. The rulers knew the doctrine of the transmigration of souls, or reincarnation, when the priests were ignorant of it.

It may well be that by inter-marriage with native peoples of India, Indus Valley and other populations, these Aryan warriors had absorbed ancient Indian ideas which were unknown to the more racially exclusive Brahmin priests. Certainly the Vedic hymns had no trace of this belief in transmigration, and in the Upanishads it is specifically stated that the Brahmins learnt it from the rulers.

The Upanishads ask many questions and they formulate problems that have remained with philosophy ever since. It has been said, with exaggeration, that European philosophy consists of footnotes to Plato, but it would be more true that Indian philosophy consists of footnotes to the Upanishads, for countless commentaries have discussed them right down to modern times. They pose original questions, such as those given by the great sage Shveta-shvatara: What is the cause of everything? Where did we come from? By what power do we live? Is it Time that was the cause? or Nature? or Fate? or Accident? or a combination of these?

The conclusion is that none of these material things can provide a satisfactory solution of the origins of the world because of the existence of the soul. This is from one of the later of the classical Upanishads, but discussion about the soul had taken place from the beginning of these dialogues. The most famous philosopher, Yajnya-valkya, had expounded this theme to his wife as he was leaving for the forest.

'Soul' is the translation of the Sanskrit word *atman*, which is derived from a root meaning 'to breathe' and related to the German *atmen*, 'breathe' and the Greek *atmos* for 'vapour' and so indirectly to the English 'atmosphere'. The sense of breath is behind this word and Breath of Life (*prana*) is another term often used in somewhat similar sense. *Atman* is translated 'self' by some writers, but in English this may suggest a too personal and even egotistical sense for this word which is far wider. The soul is the inner self of a human being but it is not ultimately individual. When Yajnya-valkya told his wife that a husband is not loved for the sake of a husband but for the sake of the soul, he was clearly indicating a being beyond any ego or self, an inner and universal essence.

The soul is not only the human soul but the universal soul, and this brings further complication. When the sage Uddalaka instructed his son in the nature of reality, in a famous series of examples that deeply influenced later Hindu philosophy, he concluded by identifying individual and universal souls: 'that subtle essence is the Soul of the whole universe. That is Reality. That is the Soul. *You* are That.'

This does not mean that there are two entities, the human soul and the divine or cosmic soul, but that they are the same and identical. Such a doctrine appeared again when Uddalaka challenged Yajnya-valkya to describe the Inner Controller, that by which one would know the world, the gods, the soul and everything. The sage answered in a number of statements which identified the power in all places and objects and beings as 'your Soul', or the self within you, which is the Inner Controller, the Immortal.

11

The Upanishads often use another term, Brahman, which is very important for Hindu philosophy but difficult to translate. The root meant 'to grow' or 'increase', and when used about sounds it meant 'to roar' as when referring to the great roar of an elephant. The meaning of increase, energy, power, makes Brahman into 'holy power' in the Vedas, especially when used of a powerful word or holy utterance. Then it became the power in the earth, in the universe, and in man himself who is 'the city of Brahman'. It is hardly surprising that quite often Brahman means the same as *atman* in the Upanishads, since the cosmic soul or being is the same as the essence of the human soul or being. Indeed the identification of Brahman and *atman*, of universal and individual souls, is said to be one of the great achievements of the Upanishads, though it is not taught everywhere or consistently. So the sage Shandilya taught: 'this soul of mine within the heart is Brahman, when I die I shall merge into it'.

In English translation one can use only approximate terms in trying to make this term Brahman comprehensible, and yet this must be attempted for the sake of the general reader. Brahman may be called Holy Power, the All, the World Ground, or the Absolute, but these are abstract and philosophical terms and cumbersome to use together. If one were to say Mind, that might make the unity of human and cosmic minds more understandable, but it might also suggest too intellectual and particular a human faculty. So the word Being has been chosen here to represent this universal power and presence. True there are other terms for Being, such as 'existence' (*sat*), as when Uddalaka asks his son, 'How can Being come out of Non-being?' But it is clear that existence is meant, though perhaps with a wider hint of the universal Being.

Another term used in the Upanishads is Purusha, which is translated by some writers as 'Person' and by others as 'Spirit', but the first of these seems too limited and individual and the second too vague. It is true that Purusha can mean simply 'man', but it is also used in the universal sense just like Brahman. It must be translated according to the sense, and generally I prefer Being for this word also, although it is often ambiguous. When Gargya talked with the King of Benares he identified the Purusha with Brahman, and the king proceeded to speak of the Soul (*atman*).

The Upanishads have often been said to teach pantheism, that everything is divine or God, and it may well be asked whether the apparent identification of the human and cosmic beings left any room for dialogue or relationships between human and divine, soul and God. It must be remembered on the one hand that we are dealing with abstract ideas and philosophy, not with popular worship of a deity. On the other hand, these sages of the Upanishads seek to prove their theories by experience and do not just put them forward for intellectual amusement. They seek to merge into That Being, to know and so to control the universal power. This is not knowledge for its own sake, but for the attainment of freedom from sorrow,

13

sickness and death itself. By mystical identification with the One, man felt that he might know the truth of the whole universe and himself become omnipotent.

However, the Upanishads are not consistently pantheistic or monistic, stating that all is divine or one. Some later philosophers pointed out that even the most monistic phrase: 'You are That' held two terms in relationship, 'you' and 'That'. To say that 'I am everything' or 'everything is God', may be not only untrue and absurd but meaningless. For if everything is identical, then nothing can be said about it that is not mere tautology. Knowledge demands difference as well as relationship.

As the Upanishads proceeded some teachers saw the need for clearer teaching about the Supreme Being as God. In recent years, in the West, there have been some efforts at modifying ideas about God as a personal deity, a being 'up there' or an 'old man in the sky'. It is suggested that we should look for a World Ground, in 'the depth of our being', though depth is just as much a spatial metaphor as height. But in India more strenuous efforts have been made than anywhere else to get away from concrete expressions into abstractions, in Power, Being, That. Yet finally some thinkers found this not satisfying intellectually and even less helpful religiously. So Shveta-shvatara found the solution to his problems of the origins of things in 'the power of God concealed in his attributes'. It is 'the greatness of God in the world that causes the wheel of Being to revolve'. It is the one God 'who spins out threads from himself like a spider', who is the cause of all, the sustainer of all, the ruler of matter and spirit, and the cause of the round of transmigration.

Another great problem that is considered from different angles in the Upanishads is that of death. Belief in some form of survival of death is probably mankind's oldest religious belief and traces of it may be seen in the way men buried their dead hundreds of thousands of years ago, with tools and weapons for the afterlife. In modern times Western thinkers have neglected the problems of death and survival, perhaps because the old symbolism of heaven and hell seemed outdated, and also because of the difficulty of formulating new theories or credible symbolism. But quite recently there has appeared a spate of studies about death, and this suggests that the gap has been found too great and that the violent nature of the modern world is forcing men to take death seriously again.

In the Vedic hymns life after death was pictured as a realm under the control of Yama, the first man who died and later the king of death, and Death himself. This Death discussed philosophical problems with young Nachiketas in the Upanishads, where, in an amusing introduction, it is said that Death was away from home for three days when the youth arrived and so had to offer him three boons in recompense.

The Upanishadic seers begin their explorations carefully. When Arta-bhaga asked what remains when a man dies, Yajnya-valkya told him in secret that deeds (*karma*) remain; this was almost a negative Buddhist answer. When he had silenced all the other sages Yajnya-valkya put them a question in the form of a poem about a tree, which has an uncanny resemblance to the comparison of man and tree in the book of Job (chapter 14). The conclusion seemed to be that 'once born man is not born again'. But later on Yajnya-valkya compared the dying soul with a caterpillar reaching the end of a blade of grass and drawing itself up to pass on to another blade, or a piece of gold which is made into another shape as the soul changes into another body.

It was young Shveta-ketu, son of Uddalaka, who was stumped by questions from an assembly of rulers when he was asked: Where do creatures go when they die? Why is the world beyond not full up? How do they come back again? The sage Uddalaka himself admitted his ignorance and was told that such know-ledge belonged to the ruling class and not to the priests. Then he was given the explanation that some souls go to heaven and do not return, but others after receiving their reward come back in the rain and are born in plants and men. The next life is determined by conduct in the past, and so they are born into noble or degraded families or even into animals by the effect of their past actions (*karma*).

This is the doctrine of transmigration or reincarna-tion and it is basic to Indian thought. If it was unknown to the Vedas and Aryan priests, it is likely that it was held by earlier Indian populations. It is believed in today not only by Hindus but by Buddhists, Jains and Sikhs and it influences other minority religions in India. Buddhist missionaries took this belief right across Asia, where it established itself in China and

Japan, despite initial difficulties, and became part of the general outlook.

Reincarnation has not been held much in the Western world, though some of the Greek philosophers believed in it and some modern poets have toyed with the idea. It seems to make a greater appeal today because of the collapse of other symbols of the afterlife. In India and most of Asia reincarnation is taken for granted; it is not argued but accepted as a fact of life. The objection raised by Westerners that memory is lacking, and that if we cannot remember our past lives there is nothing to be learnt for progress in a new life, is not fatal to the doctrine. The Upanishads say nothing about memory of past lives, and Plato in his *Republic* said that souls drink of a river of forgetfulness before being born again.

The basic argument for both survival of death and reincarnation, is the indestructible nature of the soul. This is what Death told young Nachiketas. The youth asked Death, rather curiously: 'There are doubts about the fate of a dying man. Some say that he exists, and others that he does not. What is there in the great passing-on?' Death tried to avoid giving an answer, saying that even the gods had doubts about it and offering Nachiketas wealth and women and long life instead. But when he persisted, Death declared that the soul 'never dies and is never born' because it is eternal and unslayable. 'It does not kill and is not killed,' a crucial statement which is quoted with great effect in the later and popular Bhagavad Gita.

There are other themes in the Upanishads. There is

17

the sacred syllable or *mantra* OM, a mystical utterance that was repeated or hummed to help in meditation. It was given many meanings, and one dialogue says that there is a lower OM of religious actions and a higher OM which leads through meditation to the Supreme Being. Then there is the discipline of Yoga, which was taught both by Death and by Shveta-shvatara. Yoga is related to our English word 'yoke' and like that it has a double reference, as well as various other shades of meaning. It is 'yoking' in the sense of discipline, as the control of body, mind and soul. But it is also 'yoking' in the sense of uniting, and it brings union with the divine. The Yogi 'comes to know the unborn, stable and pure Being, beyond all nature, and knowing God he is freed from all bonds'.

Other subjects are discussed in the Upanishads which the reader can study or pass by. They are often put in the context of a narrative, or attached to a particular sage, so that they are truth embodied in a tale. These stories and dialogues reveal not only that the sages of the Upanishads were philosophers, but that they had other qualities. Yajnya-valkya was a considerable poet, as witness the verses on man and tree. Many later teachings are in verse, though I have not usually attempted an English poetical equivalent, since it seemed that the meaning would be expressed more clearly in prose.

There is also considerable humour in the Upanishads. Yajnya-valkya tells his pupils to drive away the cows, not only because he claims to be the best scholar but because he wants cows. And when King Janaka later asks this teacher it he wants subtle arguments or cows, he answers 'both', though he qualifies this by saying that his father had taught him not to accept gifts without giving instruction. Elsewhere he reduced the number of gods from thousands to one and a half. Opponents were often told that if they did not accept the truth their heads would fall off, and Vidagdha's head did fall off and robbers stole his bones thinking they were something valuable.

The sages meditated upon the mystical syllable OM but Baka saw dogs moving backwards and forwards like holy beggars and howling OM, 'give us food'. Modern reciters of OM and other *mantras* might note the mockery of vain repetition. Then there are subtle digs at the wealthy Jana-shruti who built many rest-houses and provided food but heard the swan comparing him unfavourably with Raikva who lived underneath a cart scratching his itching scabs. When Jana-shruti came offering great wealth for his knowledge Raikva called him a serf, but when the rich man brought his daughter Raikva said that her face alone would make him speak.

Ushasti was another poor sage who accepted beans when hungry, against the rules of purity, but when he was offered water he refused it because water could be had anywhere. Then he went off to a king who was ordering a sacrifice, stopped the priests while they had a philosophical discussion, then allowed them to continue provided he received the same payment as they did.

Gods and demons appear as dwellers in the forest or near to men, and readers of T. S. Eliot's *Waste Land* will recognize the words of 'What the thunder said' in *Da, Da, Da* (section XXXIV). His threefold *Shantih*, 'peace' comes later (XCV). Not only gods but animals talk to men. Jana-shruti heard what the swans cried to each other. Satya-kama, who had proved his integrity, was instructed by the bull of his herd, the fire, a swan and a diver-bird. His pupil Upakosala was taught by the sacrificial fires.

Many sages and pupils are named in the Upanishads and pride of place goes to Yajnya-valkya, who occupies most of the first and oldest Great Forest Upanishad, and he should surely be recognized as one of the greatest philosophers of all time, at least an Indian Socrates or Plato. Although opposing him Uddalaka both learnt the secret of transmigration from the princes and also taught his son Shveta-ketu the great monistic doctrine, in nine parables of which five are given here. It seems that Uddalaka also was the rather niggardly or ambitious sacrificer whose more pious son, Nachiketas, bothered his father to sacrifice him as a true gift. Whether a real human sacrifice was involved here, in an Indian version of Abraham and Isaac, or whether it indicated a journey to the world beyond from which the boy returned, like Odysseus and Orpheus, is not clear. But Uddalaka lost his temper and snarled, 'I'll give you to Death', meaning, 'Oh, go to Hades'.

Angiras was another sage who had received both the lower wisdom of ritual and the higher wisdom of the

Imperishable Being. Then there was the sage Pippalada who answered the questions of six students on
the universal Being. This comes from a Upanishad
whose very name means 'Question' (*Prashna*) and
another is called 'By What?' (*Kena*) from the queries
with which it opens. We have seen that Shveta-
shvatara asks many questions and this inquiring
attitude is characteristic of the Upanishads as a whole.
Many answers are given, and they do not always
agree, but it is recognized that truth is complex. In the
same way there are several statements about the
origin of things, 'In the beginning', but they differ
and are not dogmatic assertions. In many ways the
Upanishads are intuitions rather than dogma or even
than logical constructions. There is plenty of analysis,
and enumeration of the many aspects of the world and
the human body, but the assertions at the end, 'that is
the Soul' or 'Being', come from an intuitive faith that
this is the final essence of things.

The wisdom of forest and village is a work of understanding and intuition. It is meant for consideration
and meditation. This is the truth, it says, and this leads
to wisdom, but it is cryptic rather than obvious. It is
an inner knowledge, not to be revealed to those who
are not serious students or high-spirited, pearls not to
be cast before swine.

The Upanishads, we have remarked, are not easy
reading, both from style and contents. Many readers
must have come to more formal and full translations
and soon given up in despair because they seemed
incomprehensible. In this new version I have tried to

21

make things as plain as possible, in straightforward English and using the narratives fully. Some passages have been shortened and some of the repetition reduced. But in the main this book presents the most important teachings and nearly all the narrative, as faithfully as may be. With few exceptions the order followed is that of most editions of the Upanishads and a list of references at the end indicates the location of the passages chosen.

It is hoped that this edition of the wisdom of the forest, the major teachings and stories of the classical Upanishads, will reveal the profundity of the debates in the Golden Age of the seventh century B.C., and serve as an aid to reflection on questions which have concerned all ages of mankind.

SAGES OF THE INDIAN
UPANISHADS

* I *

IN THE Great Forest Treatise this prayer is given to be murmured as an introductory purification:

> From Unreality lead me to Reality,
> From Darkness lead me to Enlightenment,
> From Death lead me to Immortality.

* II *

YAJNYA-VALKYA, one of the greatest sages, was about to change from the life of a householder to the stage of dwelling in the forest. He had two wives, one was only interested in women's affairs but the other, Maitreyi, liked philosophical discussion. Maitreyi, he said, I am leaving home and I want to make a settlement for you both. But Maitreyi replied: If the whole world and its riches were mine, would that make me immortal? No, he said, you would live the life of the rich, but that would give no hope of immortality. Maitreyi asked: What is the use of something that could not make me immortal? Tell me rather everything you know.

* III *

YAJNYA-VALKYA told his wife that he loved her and her words were lovely. He asked her to sit down so that she could ponder the matter while he explained it. Then he said: Truly a husband is not loved for the love of a husband but he is loved for the sake of the Soul. In fact a wife is not loved for the love of a wife but she is loved for the sake of the Soul. Indeed sons are not loved for the love of sons but they are loved for the sake of the Soul. He enumerated all the things that men seem to love: riches, property, class, the worlds, the gods, the scriptures, and all beings. Verily, he said, all things are not loved for the love of all but all are loved for the sake of the Soul. O Maitreyi, the Soul is that which should be perceived and heard and thought about and meditated upon. In perceiving the Soul, listening to it, thinking about it, and understanding it, the whole universe is understood.

* IV *

KING BRIHAD-RATHA, a powerful hero, had meditated upon the decaying nature of the body and become indifferent to life in the world. When his son came of age he appointed him ruler over the kingdom and retired into the heart of the forest. There the former king practised extreme asceticism, raising his arms in the air while he gazed at the sun. After a thousand days the ascetic was approached by the Master Shaka-yanya, one who understood the Soul. He arrived like a smokeless fire, glowing with heat, and said to the king: Get up, ask me a favour. The king put his hands together at his forehead in obeisance and confessed: Sir, I cannot understand the Soul. We have heard that you comprehend its nature, so please instruct me. Shaka-yanya replied: People used to know about this matter, but it is very difficult to explain, ask me something else.

★ V ★

BRIHAD-RATHA bowed down his head until it touched the sage's feet and uttered this complaint on the state of worldly life: Sir, this body is smelly and weak, made up of bone, skin, muscle, flesh, marrow, blood, semen, mucus, tears, bile, excreta and wind. What pleasure is there in these? This body is attacked by anger, lust, greed, delusion, fear, despair, envy, hunger, thirst, disease, sorrow, old age and death. What pleasure is there in these? The whole world is decaying, like gnats and flies, grass and trees, that rise only to perish. Seas dry up, mountain peaks crumble, stars move away, winds are unleashed, the earth sinks and the gods disappear. What good are pleasures in this cycle of existence, when man tastes them but comes back to earth again and again? Please save me, for in this round of existence I am like a frog in a waterless well. You alone have the way of escape.

★ VI ★

SHAKA-YANYA was pleased and told the king: You are a great hero, you will quickly achieve your purpose, be renowned as the wind, and become a Knower of the Soul. Indeed that is your own self. The king asked: Which self is that? Shaka-yanya replied: It is he who, without causing the breath to stop, rises up on high. He moves about yet is motionless. He dispels darkness —that is the Soul. This is what the sages have taught:

The Soul is that serene one who rises up from the body, attains the highest light and appears there in its own form. That is the immortal. That is the fearless. That is true Being.

GARGYA was a learned sage who went to Ajata-shatru, king of Benares, and said: Shall I tell you about Holy Power, the cosmic Being? The king replied: Yes indeed. If you do so I will give you a thousand cows and people will say that my generosity is like that of King Janaka. Gargya said: It is the Spirit in the sun that I worship as Being. But Ajata-shatru protested: Do not talk of him like that, for I worship him already as the lord and head and king of all creatures, who gives eminence to his worshippers. Gargya said: It is the Spirit in the moon that I worship as Being. The king said: Do not talk of him like that, for I worship him already as the great white-robed monarch, who gives nourishment to his worshippers. Then Gargya named the Spirit in lightning, space, wind, fire, earth, mirror, sound, heavens, shadow and body as the Being that is to be worshipped. But each time the king countered his claim. Finally Gargya was silent and Ajata-shatru asked: Have you done? Gargya replied: I have done. The king said: That is not enough for true knowledge.

GARGYA SAID: Let me learn from you. King Ajata-shatru answered: It is not normal for a priest to come to a ruler to learn about Being. However, I will make you understand clearly. He took his hand and they went to a man who was asleep. The two of them spoke to the sleeper: Get up, O great king! But he did not rise till Ajata-shatru woke him up by rubbing his hand. Then Ajata-shatru asked: When this man was sleeping where was his intelligent Spirit? Where did he come back from? But Gargya did not know. The king continued: When a man is asleep the intelligent Spirit rests in the space within the heart. The breath, voice, eye, ear and mind are restrained. When he is asleep the dream worlds are his, and there he becomes like a great king or a priest, entering high and low places, and moving around in his body as he pleases.

As a spider puts out threads from itself, or as sparks shoot out of a fire, so all vital breaths, all worlds, all gods and beings come forth from the Soul. The mystical meaning of this is—the Real of the real. The breaths of life are real, the Soul is their reality.

* IX *

KING AJATA-SHATRU said: When a man wakes up his bodily powers return to their respective places, as sparks are scattered from a blazing fire. The intelligent Soul enters the body up to the hair and the finger-tips. As a razor fits into a razor-case, or as a fire fills a brazier, so the intelligent Soul enters the body. Men cannot see the Soul, for if he were to be seen he would be incomplete. In breathing his name is breath; in speaking his name is voice, in seeing his name is the eye; in hearing his name is the ear; in thinking his

27

name is the mind. But these are simply the names of his actions. Whoever worships any one of these has no right knowledge, for he is incomplete in each one. Let a man worship him as the Soul, in which all these parts become one. As one might find a man by his footprints, so the Soul is a trace of everything, for by it one knows the whole universe.

* X *

JANAKA, KING OF VIDEHA, prepared a sacrifice at which large fees were to be paid. Many sages were invited and the king wanted to discover which was the most learned. He herded together a thousand cows, with ten gold pieces tied to the horns of each. Venerable sages, he said, let the wisest scholar among you drive away these cows. But those sages dared not do so. Then Yajnya-valkya said to his pupil: Drive them away, my dear. The other seers protested: How dare he claim to be the best scholar? Janaka's own priest inquired: Are you really the best scholar among us, Yajnya-valkya? He replied: We should revere the best scholar, but I just want to have those cows.

* XI *

THE SAGES began to question Yajnya-valkya one by one and he answered them in a series of philosophical tournaments. The wise Arta-bhaga asked him: When a man dies, what is there that does not leave him? Yajnya-valkya replied: The name. For the name is endless, and the gods are infinite, and by knowing this man gains the infinite world of heaven. Arta-bhaga asked: When a man dies, if his voice enters the fire, and his breath goes into wind, his eyes into the sun, his mind into the moon, his hearing into the heavens, his body into the earth, his soul into space, his hairs into plants, his blood and seed into water—where is that person then? Yajnya-valkya answered: Take my hand, my friend. We will discuss this alone for we should not talk of it in public. They went away and spoke together, and what they talked about was action (*karma*). What they praised was action. For one becomes good by good action and evil by evil action.

* XII *

THEN USHASTA questioned him: Explain to me that present and evident Being which is the Soul in everything. Yajnya-valkya answered: It is your Soul which is in everything. He asked: But what kind of Soul is in everything? He replied: That which breathes in with every breath is your Soul which is in everything. That which breathes out, about and up, is your Soul which is in everything. Ushasta protested: You have described this like someone who says: That is a cow and this is a horse. But show me that present and evident Being which is the Soul in everything. Yajnya-valkya retorted: You cannot see the seer of seeing! You cannot think the thinker of thinking! You cannot understand the understander of understanding! That is your Soul which is in everything.

KAHOLA questioned Yajnya-valkya: Explain to me that present and evident Being which is the Soul in everything. He replied: It is your Soul which is in everything. Kahola asked: But what kind of Soul is in everything! Yajnya-valkya answered: The one that is beyond hunger and thirst, sorrow and delusion, age and death. When scholars know this Soul they pass beyond desire for sons or wealth or heavenly worlds and they wander away to live as forest ascetics. For a desire for sons is a desire for wealth, and a desire for wealth is a desire for all the worlds, since both are desires. Indeed a wise man should renounce learning and live like a child. And when he has renounced both learning and childlike simplicity then he becomes a silent sage. And when he renounces both sound and silence then he is a mystic who knows reality.

THERE WERE WOMEN sages and Gargi, daughter of Vachaknu, questioned Yajnya-valkya. She said: Since all the universe is woven on water, on what is water woven? He replied: On wind. On what is wind woven? On air. On what is air woven? On the sky. On what is the sky woven? On the sun. On what is the sun woven? On the worlds of the gods. On what are the worlds of the gods woven? Yajnya-valkya concluded: Do not ask too many questions, Gargi, or your head will fall off. You are asking too much about cosmic powers concerning which further questions may not be asked.

UDDALAKA, a famous sage, said to Yajnya-valkya: Once we were staying with Kapya, studying the sacrifice, and his wife was possessed by a spirit. We asked this spirit his name and he replied by telling Kapya to identify that thread on which this world and the next and all beings are strung together. Kapya had to admit that he did not know this and the spirit then asked him and us if we knew that Inner Controller which from within governs the worlds and all things. Kapya again replied that he did not know it and the spirit answered that he who knows that uniting thread and that Inner Controller understands Being. He knows the worlds, the gods, the scriptures, the creatures, the Soul and everything, This was explained to us, and I know it.

UDDALAKA warned Yajnya-valkya: If you drive those cows away without knowing the Inner Controller your head will fall off. He replied: I do know that Inner Controller. Uddalaka retorted: Anybody could say 'I know, I know'. Tell us what you know. Yajnya-valkya began: That which is in the earth but is different from the earth, which the earth does not know, which has the earth as body and controls it from within—that is your Soul, the Inner Controller, the Immortal. That which is in water but is different from water, which water does not know, which has water as body and controls it from within—that is your Soul, the Inner Controller, the Immortal. That which is in fire but is different from fire, which fire does not know, which has fire as body and controls it from within—that is your Soul, the Inner Controller, the Immortal. Yajnya-valkya proceeded by identifying the Inner Controller in the air, wind, sky, sun, heavens, moon, stars, space, darkness, light, breath, speech, eye, ear, mind, skin, understanding and seed. Then he concluded, Uddalaka being silent: He is the unseen Seer, the unheard Hearer, the unthought Thinker, the unknown Knower. There is no other Seer, Hearer, Thinker or Knower. That is your Soul, the Inner Controller, the Immortal.

* XVII *

THE WOMAN GARGI questioned Yajnya-valkya again: That which is above the sky, beneath the earth, and between these two, which men call the past and present and future, on what is that woven? He replied: That is what wise men call the Imperishable. It is not coarse or fine, short or long, hot or wet. It has no shadow or darkness, no air or space. It has no attachment, taste or smell. It is not eye or ear, voice or mind, light or breath. It has no face or name, no within or without. It consumes nothing and nothing consumes it. Yajnya-valkya said moreover: Truly the sun and moon are held apart at the command of this Imperishable Being, and so are minutes and hours, days and nights, months and years. At the command of that Imperishable Being some rivers flow eastwards from the snowy mountains and others westwards. Indeed if a man offers sacrifices or alms, or performs austerities for thousands of years

32

but does not know that Imperishable Being his work is limited. Whoever dies without knowing the Imperishable Being is miserable, but one who dies knowing the Imperishable Being is a true sage.

⋆ XVIII ⋆

VIDAGDHA questioned Yajnya-valkya: How many gods are there? He replied: In the Hymn to All the Gods three thousand three hundred and six are mentioned. Yes, but how many gods are there really? Thirty-three. Yes, but how many gods are there really? Six. Yes, but how many gods are there really? Three. Yes, but how many gods are there really? Two. Yes, but how many gods are there really? One and a half. Yes, but how many gods are there really? One. What is the one God? The Breath of Life, Being, they call it That.

⋆ XIX ⋆

VIDAGDHA said: Yajnya-valkya, since you have claimed to surpass all these scholars in debate, what is the holy knowledge that you have? He replied: I know all the powers of all regions. Vidagdha asked: Tell us where these powers are. Yajnya-valkya retorted: You are a fool if you think that this power is anywhere else but in ourselves. If it were anywhere else the dogs might eat it or the birds might tear it to bits. The Soul is not this, not that. It cannot be grasped, bound or destroyed. That is the Spirit taught in the secret sessions about whom I am telling you. If you cannot understand it, your head will fall off. Vidagdha did not understand this and his head fell off. Then robbers carried his bones away, thinking they were something valuable.

* XX *

AFTER these debates Yajnya-valkya concluded: Reverend scholars, if anyone else wants to question me let him do so. All of you question me, or I will question one or all of you. But none of those sages dared ask any more questions and so he put his own question in these verses:

> King of the forest, like a tree,
> is surely what a man should be—
> the leaves are like the body's hairs
> and outer bark with skin compares.
>
> The blood runs underneath the skin
> as sap moves through the trunk within
> and sap when he is wounded flows
> as from a tree when struck by blows.
>
> But any tree when it is felled
> grows from the root as new impelled;
> yet mortal man, when felled by death,
> what root can nourish further breath?
>
> Say not 'the seed' which can derive
> its power only from the live,
> and trees when pulled up by the roots
> can never more produce their shoots.
>
> Once born, man is not born again,
> for who begets the one that's slain?

34

But Being is wisdom, joyful bliss,
the goal of gifts and of one who is
established firm by knowing This.

YAJNYA-VALKYA returned to King Janaka and found
him sitting on a couch. The king asked him: Why
have you come to me? Do you want subtle arguments
or do you want cows? Both, your majesty, he retorted.
But let me hear what other sages have told you. Well,
said the king, one told me that Being is speech.
Yajnya-valkya replied: That is obvious. It is like
saying that a man had a mother or a father or a teacher,
for what use is a man without speech? But did he tell
you its support and basis? No, he did not tell me. Then
he is a scholar who only stands on one leg. The king
said: You must tell me the truth, and I will give you
a thousand cows with a bull as big as an elephant.
Yajnya-valkya answered: My father warned me not
to accept gifts without giving true instruction. What
have other teachers told you? The king replied that
five scholars had identified Being with breath, eye, ear,
mind and heart. But Yajnya-valkya declared that these
were only partially true and did not show its support
and basis. The king offered him thousands of cows but
the sage declined until he had given true instruction.

KING JANAKA came down from his throne, put his
folded hands to his head in salutation, and asked
Yajnya-valkya to teach him. The sage said: As a king

35

about to go on a long journey would prepare a carriage or a ship, so your soul has been prepared by these mystical doctrines. Since you are so eminent and wealthy, learned in the scriptures and versed in mystical doctrines, tell me, where will you go when you depart from this world? The king replied: I do not know where I shall go. Yajnya-valkya said: Then I will teach you, but cryptically, for the gods love the cryptic and dislike the obvious.

* XXIII *

YAJNYA-VALKYA said: The Soul is not this or that. It is intangible, for it cannot be grasped. It is indestructible, for it cannot be destroyed. It is detached, for it cannot be attached. It is not bound, it does not tremble, it cannot be hurt.

* XXIV *

ON ANOTHER OCCASION Yajnya-valkya visited King Janaka but thought to himself: I will not speak to him. Later on, when a sacrifice had been offered, the sage offered the king a wish and he asked these questions. The king said: What is the light of man? He replied: It is the sun, for by its light he sits down, moves about, works and goes home. The king asked: But when the sun has set, what is the light of man? Yajnya-valkya answered: It is the moon, for by its light he sits down, moves about, works and goes home. But when the sun and the moon have set, what is the light of man? It is fire, for by its light he sits down, moves about, works and goes home. But when the sun and moon have set and the fire has gone out, what is the light of man? It is speech, for by its light he sits down, moves about, works and goes home. But when the sun and moon have set, the fire has gone out, and speech is hushed, what is the light of man? The Soul is his light. For it is by the light of the Soul that one sits down, moves about, works and goes home.

* XXV *

KING JANAKA asked: What is the Soul? Yajnya-valkya replied: It is that Spirit among the senses which consists of intelligence and is the Inner Light in the heart. It lives in two worlds, seeming to think and seeming to move about. When it sleeps it transcends this world. When this Spirit is born into a body it is linked with evil things, but when it goes away at death it leaves evil behind. There are two states of this Spirit, in this world and the next. But there is an intermediate state which is sleep. In that state one sees both the others, this world and the next.

* XXVI *

YAJNYA-VALKYA analysed the dream state of the creative spirit: When one falls asleep he takes materials from this world, breaking them down and building them up again, dreaming by his own radiance and light. So this Spirit is self-illuminated. In the dream state there are no chariots, animals or roads, but one projects chariots, animals and roads from oneself. There are no joys, pleasures or delights in the dream world, but one projects joys, pleasures and delights

37

from oneself. There are no pools, lakes and rivers in the dream world, but one projects pools, lakes and rivers from oneself, for the Spirit is a creator. There is a verse on this subject:

> Subduing the bodily state with sleep,
> sleepless he looks upon those who sleep,
> assuming light he returns therefrom,
> the Golden Spirit, the Lonely Swan.

> People may see his pleasure-ground
> but he himself is never found.

⋆ XXVII ⋆

KING JANAKA was pleased with these words and said: That is true. I will give you a thousand cows. Tell me the higher knowledge which leads to liberation. Yajnya-valkya gave a number of examples of the state of the Spirit in sleep and waking. As a great fish swims from one bank of a river to the other, so the Spirit roams through both sleeping and waking states. As a falcon or an eagle flies around in space, and when it is tired it folds its wings and settles down on its nest, so the Spirit hastens to the state of dreamless sleep where there are no desires. As a man in the embrace of his beloved wife knows nothing without or within, so a man embraced by the intelligent Soul knows nothing without or within.

⋆ XXVIII ⋆

YAJNYA-VALKYA spoke about death in similes: As a cart when it is heavily loaded starts creaking, so the bodily self starts groaning when the intelligent Soul has mounted upon it. As a mango or a fig or a berry detaches itself from its stalk, so when the bodily self wastes away through age or sickness, it detaches itself from its limbs and returns to its origin, to the breath of life. As policemen, magistrates, charioteers and village leaders wait for the arrival of a king, with food and drink and lodging, and cry 'He is coming, here he is'; so all the bodily elements gather round the man who has this knowledge and cry 'He is coming, here he is.' As policemen, magistrates, charioteers and village leaders gather round a king when he is leaving, so the vital powers gather round the Soul when a man breathes his last.

⋆ XXIX ⋆

YAJNYA-VALKYA spoke again about death: When the bodily self becomes weak and confused, then the vital powers gather round it. They say: He is becoming one, he cannot see. He is becoming one, he cannot smell or taste or speak or hear or think or feel or understand. The tip of the heart lights up and by this light the Soul departs, through the eye or the head or some other part of the body. As it departs the life goes out and after the life the breaths go out. Consciousness follows and he becomes one with intelligence. His knowledge and deeds and memory take hold of him.

⋆ XXX ⋆

YAJNYA-VALKYA spoke of the Soul taking a new form: As a caterpillar comes to the end of a blade of grass and draws itself together for the next step, so the Soul rids itself of the body, dispels its ignorance, and draws itself together for another life. As a goldsmith takes a piece of gold and makes another and more beautiful form, so the Soul rids itself of the body, dispels its ignorance and makes for itself another and more beautiful form. The slough of a snake may be seen lying cast off and dead on an ant-hill, and so this body lies cast off. But the bodiless and immortal Spirit is Being and light indeed. King Janaka was delighted at all these teachings and said: Noble sir, I will give you a thousand cows.

* XXXI *

YAJNYA-VALKYA spoke of the beginning: A man by himself is like half a pot, but it was not always so. In the beginning the world was the Soul alone, in the form of one man. When he looked round he only saw himself and he said 'This is I'. So the name 'I' came into being, and to this day when a man is addressed he says first 'It is I' and then what other name he has. He was afraid, for a man who is alone is afraid. But he thought: Since nothing else exists, what am I afraid of? And his fear passed away, for fear only comes from a second person. He had no pleasure, since a man who is alone has no joy and he longed for a partner. Now he was as big as a man and a woman in close embrace, so he broke himself into two parts, becoming husband and wife, and from them human beings were produced. At that time the world was undistinguished, and it became distinct in names and forms, so that men say:

40

He has this name and that form. It is by names and forms that distinctions exist in the world.

* XXXII *

YAJNYA-VALKYA prepared to return to the forest and instructed his philosopher-wife Maitreyi again: As a lump of salt dissolves in water and cannot be taken out, because it is all salty, so this great being, the Soul, which is infinite, is just a mass of intelligence. It appears with the elements and disappears with them. After death there is no separate consciousness. Maitreyi protested: Now you have confused me by saying that after death there is no consciousness. Yajnya-valkya replied: There is nothing confusing here, for the Soul is imperishable and indestructible. But where there is duality one sees somebody else, and there is duality where one smells, hears, speaks to, thinks about or understands somebody else. Yet when everything has become the Soul, who else could one see or smell? By what means could one know him by whom one knows the whole universe? By what means could one know the Knower? Yajnya-valkya said finally: Now you have had full instruction, Maitreyi. This indeed brings immortality. When he had said this Yajnya-valkya took his leave and departed into the forest.

* XXXIII *

GODS AND DEMONS, children of the Lord of Creatures, lived in the forest. The demons were older and the gods younger, and they were engaged in constant struggle for control of the worlds. The gods said: Let us conquer the demons at sacrifice with the Sacred Chant, the mystical syllable OM. They said to Speech: Sing us the OM. But the demons knew that they could be overcome and rushing on Speech they pierced it with evil, and that is why men speak evil things. The gods said to the Eye: Sing us the OM. But the demons knew they could be overcome and rushing on the Eye they pierced it with evil, and what is why men see evil things. The gods called in the same manner upon the Ear and the Mind, but the demons infected them with evil hearing and thinking. So the gods called upon the Breath of Life and when the demons rushed upon it they were scattered in all directions, like a clod of earth which is struck upon a stone. For the Breath of Life is the essence of the limbs and the lord of Speech.

* XXXIV *

THREE CHILDREN of the Lord of Creatures—gods, men and demons, lived with their father as students of sacred knowledge. After some time as students the gods said to him: Speak to us, sir. He uttered one syllable: *Da*, and asked if they understood. They replied: We did understand. You said: Restrain yourselves (*damyata*). Then the men said to him: Speak to us, sir. He uttered one syllable: *Da*, and asked if they understood. They replied: We did understand. You said: Give (*datta*). Then the demons said to him: Speak to us, sir. He uttered one syllable: *Da*, and asked if they understood. They replied: We did understand. You said: Be compassionate (*dayadhvam*). This is how the divine voice rolls in the thunder: *Da, Da, Da.* Restrain yourselves, give, be compassionate. One should practise this threefold command: Self-restraint, giving, compassion.

⋆ XXXV ⋆

ONCE UPON A TIME the organs of the body were debating among themselves which was the greatest, each saying in turn: I am the best. I am the best. They went to their father, the Lord of Creatures, and asked him: Sir, which is the best of us? He replied: That one which leaves the body the worst off when it goes away. So Speech went away and after a year it came back and asked the other organs: How did you get on without me? They answered: We were like the dumb not speaking, but we breathed with breath, we saw with the eye, we heard with the ear, we knew with the mind. Therefore Speech entered the body again. Then the Eye went away and after a year it came back and asked the other organs: How did you get on without me? They answered: We were like the blind not seeing, but we breathed with breath, we spoke with speech, we heard with the ear, we knew with the mind. Therefore the Eye entered the body again. Then in turn the Ear and the Mind went away and on returning found that the other organs had managed without them. Finally the Breath of Life prepared to go away. As a great horse might pull up the pegs that tether it to the ground, so the Breath of Life prepared to pull away all the other organs. But all the organs united and said: Sir, do not go away for we cannot live without you.

You are the best of us. You are as excellent as Speech, as firm a basis as the Eye, as successful as the Ear, as homely as the Mind. All these bodily organs are called breaths, for the Breath of Life is all these.

* XXXVI *

THE LORD OF CREATURES was brooding over the worlds and as he brooded there came forth threefold knowledge in the sacred scriptures. He brooded further and there came the threefold regions of earth, air and sky in three syllables. He brooded on these also and out of them came forth the sacred syllable OM. As leaves may be held together by a stake so all speech is held together by OM. Indeed OM is the whole universe. Yes, OM is the whole universe.

* XXXVII *

THREE MEN were discussing the Sacred Chant, the OM. Shilaka and Chikitana were priests and Pravahana was a prince. As they sat down the latter said: You two speak first, sirs, for while two priests discuss the matter I will listen. So Shilaka began: What is the essence of OM? Chikitana replied: It is sound. What is the essence of sound? It is breath. What is the essence of breath? It is food. What is the essence of food? It is water. What is the essence of water? It is the heavenly world, said Chikitana. We cannot go beyond the heavenly world. So we have found the essence and support of the Sacred Chant and we praise it as heaven. But Shilaka protested: The heavenly world leads back to this world and the Sacred Chant is the support of this

world. Then Pravahana interrupted: But this world comes to an end and your argument fails. Shilaka asked: Tell me then, sir, what is the essence and support of this world? He answered: It is space. For all creatures come out of space and they return into space. Space alone is greater than everything, and space is the supreme support and final goal.

* XXXVIII *

ONE DAY the sage Baka went out to a quiet place to study the scriptures. As he was there a white dog appeared and other dogs gathered round it saying: Sir, we are hungry, get food for us by singing. The white dog replied: Come to me here tomorrow morning. So Baka kept watch and next day he saw the dogs moving backwards and forwards together, as priests do when they chant hand in hand. They sat down, cleared their throats, and howled: OM, let us eat. OM, let us drink. OM, may the gods bring food here. O Lord of food bring food and bring it here. OM.

* XXXIX *

ONCE when the crops had been destroyed by hail-storms there was a very poor scholar, Ushasti, who had nothing to eat. He went to a rich man in the village and found him eating beans. Ushasti begged for food but the rich man said: I have nothing but those beans left on the plate and they would be impure to you. Ushasti pleaded: Give them to me. The rich man gave him the beans and offered water as well, saying: Here is a drink. But Ushasti refused saying: I cannot drink water that has been left by another and is impure. The rich man asked: Were not the beans also leavings and impure? No, retorted Ushasti, I needed the beans to live, but I can get water anywhere.

★ XL ★

USHASTI went home to his wife and gave her the remainder of the beans, but she had received some food from begging and put the beans away till morning. Then she put them before her husband to eat. Ushasti said: If we could get some money we could buy food. The king over there is going to have a sacrifice made and he might choose me to perform the priestly office. So he went off to where the sacrifice was being prepared and said to the three officiants: If you do this work without understanding the powers that are connected with the ritual, your heads will fall off. The priests stopped their preparations and sat down in silence. Then the priest who was to sing the Introductory Praise asked him: What is the power connected with this act? Ushasti replied: It is the Breath of Life, for all things come into life with Breath and leave it with Breath. The priest of the Chant asked: What is the power connected with this act? He said: It is the Sun, for all beings sing of the sun when it rises. The priest of the Response asked: What is the power connected with this act? He said: It is Food, for all creatures live by taking Food into themselves. Then the supervisor of the sacrifice said: I would like to know who you are, sir. He replied: I am Ushasti. The supervisor said: I have been looking for someone

46

like you to perform these sacrifices, but when I did not find him I chose others. Please take up all the priestly offices for me. Ushasti replied: Very well, but let these others sing the chants, and you must give me as much money as you give them.

THE SAGE SHANDILYA taught the famous doctrine of the identity of the individual soul with the cosmic Being. he said: Truly, all this universe is Being. One should reverence it in tranquillity, since by it we live and move and dissolve. A person consists of mind, its body is breath, its form is light, its idea is truth, its self is space. It contains all works, all desires, all perfumes, all tastes. It encompasses the whole universe, it never speaks and has no care. This Soul of mine within my heart is smaller than a grain of rice or barley or millet, or a mustard-seed or the kernel of a grain of millet. This Soul of mine within the heart is greater than the earth, greater than the air, greater than the sky, greater than all the worlds. This Soul of mine within the heart is that Being. When I leave here I shall merge into it.

KRISHNA, the 'black', a disciple of the sage Ghora, had passed beyond desire. Ghora said to him: At the hour of death one should hold fast these three thoughts: You are indestructible. You are unshakeable. You are the Breath of Life.

JANA-SHRUTI was a pious man who gave away much in alms and food. He built rest-houses everywhere, hoping that people would eat his provisions. One night two swans flew past his house and one called to the other: Hey, are you short-sighted? Take care not to touch the light of Jana-shruti, it is as wide as the sky and would burn you up. The other swan replied: Pooh, you talk of him as if he were as good as Raikva, the man with the cart. The first asked: What about Raikva, the man with the cart? The second swan answered: As all winnings go to the man who throws the highest dice, so all good deeds go to the one who knows what Raikva knows. Jana-shruti heard these words, called his servant and said: You must speak of me like Raikva, the man with the cart. The servant asked: Who is this Raikva? Jana-shruti sent him out to find Raikva, but he returned saying that he could not find him. Jana-shruti sent him again to look in those places where one might find a sage. The servant discovered a man scratching his scabs underneath a cart and asked him: Are you Raikva, sir? The sage replied: I am. The servant returned to tell his master that he had found the sage.

JANA-SHRUTI took six hundred cows, a gold necklace, and a chariot with mules and went to the sage. He said: Raikva, here are six hundred cows, a gold necklace and a chariot with mules. Please teach me about the God whom you worship. Raikva replied:

Keep your necklace and carriage and cows, you serf! Then Jana-shruti took a thousand cows, a gold necklace, a chariot with mules, and his own daughter and went to the sage. He said: Raikva, here are a thousand cows, a gold necklace, a chariot with mules, and a wife, and you can have the village where you live. Please teach me, sir. Then Raikva lifted up the girl's face and gazed at her, and said to himself: This serf has brought these cows, but this face alone would make me speak. So Raikva taught Jana-shruti, for as all winnings go to the man who throws the highest dice, so all good deeds go to the one who knows what Raikva knows. And the same is true about whoever knows what he knew.

* XLV *

THERE WAS A YOUNG MAN named Satya-kama whose mother's name was Jabala. One day he said to her: I want to live as a student of sacred knowledge, please tell me about my family. She replied: I know nothing of your family. When I was young I went about as a servant-maid and conceived you, but I do not know your father's name. You can take my name. Satya-kama went to the sage Gautama and said: I want to become your pupil, sir, as a student of sacred knowledge. Gautama asked him: What is your family, my dear? The youth replied: I do not know my parentage. My mother told me that she got me when she was a serving-maid. However, my name is Satya-kama and hers is Jabala, so I am Satya-kama Jabala. Gautama answered: Only a wise man could put it so clearly. I

49

will accept you as a pupil, if you bring the fuel which is the ancient token that you come to a teacher for instruction, for you have kept to the truth.

* XLVI *

A PUPIL was supposed to work for his teacher and when Gautama had accepted Satya-kama he chose four hundred lean and weak cows, saying: Look after these, my dear. As he drove them out Satya-kama said: I shall not come back till there are a thousand of them. So Satya-kama stayed away for a number of years till the cows reached a thousand. One day the bull of the herd spoke to him: Satya-Kama! He replied: Yes, sir. The bull said: My dear boy, there are a thousand of us now. Take us back to the teacher's house and I will tell you a quarter of the nature of Being. He said: Tell me now. The bull said: One part of it is the East, one part is the West, one part is the South, one part is the North. This quarter of Being is in four parts; it is called the Shining. Whoever knows this becomes shining in this world.

* XLVII *

THE BULL said to Satya-kama: The Fire will tell you another quarter. So next day he drove the cows on and in the evening he built a fire and sat down by it, facing east. The Fire said: Satya-kama! He replied: Yes, sir. The Fire said: I will tell you a quarter of the nature of Being. One part is the earth, one part the air, one part the sky, one part the sea. This quarter of Being is in

four parts; it is called the Infinite. Whoever knows this
becomes infinite in this world.

THE FIRE said to Satya-kama: A Swan will tell you
another quarter. So the next day he drove the cows on
and in the evening he built a fire and sat down by it, facing
east. A swan flew down to him and called: Satya-kama!
He replied: Yes, sir. The swan said: I will tell you a
quarter of the nature of Being. One part of it is fire,
one part the sun, one part the moon, one part the
lightning. This quarter of Being is in four parts; it is
called Luminous. Whoever knows this becomes
luminous in this world.

THE SWAN said to Satya-kama: A diver-bird will tell
you another quarter. So the next day he drove the
cows on and in the evening he built a fire and sat down
by it, facing east. A diver-bird flew down to him and
called: Satya-kama! He replied: Yes, sir. The diver-
bird said: I will tell you a quarter of the nature of
Being. One part of it is breath, one part is sight, one
part is hearing, one part is the mind. This quarter of
Being is in four parts; it is called the Abode. Whoever
knows this has an abode in this world.

SATYA-KAMA reached his teacher's house at last and
Gautama called to him: Satya-kama! He replied: Yes,
sir. Gautama said: My dear boy, you are as radiant as a

man who knows Being. Who has been teaching you? He admitted: It was not human beings. But it is you alone whom I would like to teach me, for I have heard from others like you that wisdom from a teacher brings the best results. Then Gautama repeated those words which the others had spoken, omitting nothing. Indeed, nothing was omitted.

* LI *

IN COURSE OF TIME Satya-kama himself became a teacher of sacred knowledge with a number of pupils. One of them, Upa-kosala, tended his fires for twelve years and the master did not allow him to go home when other pupils left. Satya-kama's wife said: This student is disciplined and tends the fires well. Why not give him full knowledge yourself, before the fires anticipate you? But Satya-kama had to go away on a journey before teaching him. Then Upa-kosala was ill and did not eat. The teacher's wife said: Young man, you must eat. Why are you not eating? He replied: Man has many desires which distract him. I am full of illness and cannot eat. Then the fires spoke among themselves, saying: This student has disciplined himself and tended us well. Come, let us teach him. They said to him: Being is the Breath of Life. Being is Joy. Being is Space. He replied: I know that the Breath of Life is Being, but I do not understand how Joy and Space are that. They said: Joy is the same as Space. Space is the same as Joy (one is *Ka*, the other is *Kha*). Then they explained the Breath of Life and Space to him.

52

THE FIRES instructed Upa-kosala in the identity of the cosmic Being in all objects. The householder's fire said: Earth, fire, food and sun are forms of me. I am indeed the Being that is seen in the sun. The southern sacrificial fire said: Water, regions, stars and moon are forms of me. I am indeed the Being that is seen in the moon. The eastern sacrificial fire said: The breath of life, space, sky and lightning are forms of me. I am indeed the Being that is seen in lightning. The fires sang together in chorus: Whoever knows and reverences this, repels evil deeds from himself, gains exalted states, and lives a long and glorious life.

THE TEACHER SATYA-KAMA returned and called: Upa-kosala! He replied: Yes, sir. Satya-kama said: My dear boy, you are as radiant as a man who knows Being. Who has been teaching you? Upa-kosala appeared to deny it, saying: Who could teach me but you, sir? These fires seem to be dull now, but they were different. Satya-kama asked: What did they teach you? Upa-kosala told him all. Then Satya-kama said: They did indeed tell you about states of being, but I will tell you something else. Evil deeds will not cling to the man who knows this, but will slip away from him as water slips off lotus leaves.

MANY of the forest sages meditated upon the origins of the universe and put forward different views. One said: In the beginning there was nothing here at all. The world was enclosed by Death, that is to say by Hunger, for Hunger is Death. Then Death thought: Let me have a self. He wandered about singing praises and as he worshipped water was produced from him. Death longed for a second self and produced Speech, by means of his mind. By his self, with Speech, he brought forth everything that exists.

YAJNYA-VALKYA said: In the beginning the world was the Soul alone (see passage XXXI). Another sage said: In the beginning this universe was Holy Power, cosmic Being, the All. It knew itself, saying: I am Being. And it became the All. If any of the gods became aware of this he also became Being, and so did sages and men. Even now this is true, that whoever knows: I am Being, becomes Being. The gods themselves cannot prevent this, for he becomes their self. In the beginning this universe was cosmic Being and single. Being one it could not develop, but by great effort it brought forth superior forms of gods and powers and common people. By another greater effort it brought forth a better form, which was the Right. Right is the power of rulers and there is nothing higher than Right. A weak man, like a king, controls a strong man by Right. Right is truth. A man who speaks the truth is said to speak Right, and a man who speaks Right is said to speak the truth, for they are the same.

ANOTHER SAGE said: There are two forms of cosmic
Being: formed and formless, mortal and immortal, still
and moving, actual and ultimate. As regards the Soul,
the 'formed' is what is different from breath and the
space within the soul. This is mortal, static and actual.
But the 'formless' is the breath and the space within
the soul. This is immortal, moving and ultimate. The
form of this Being is like a saffron-coloured robe, like
white wool, like a red beetle, like a flame of fire, like
a white lotus, like a flash of lightning. And like a flash
of lightning is the glory of the man who knows this.

ANOTHER SAGE said: In the beginning the world was
just water. Water brought forth the Real, that Being
which is Real, and then the gods were produced. The
gods worshipped the Real. The sun is the same as the
Real. The Being that is in the sun, and the Being that
is in the right eye are dependent upon one another.
Through its rays the eye depends on the sun, and
through its vital breath the sun depends on the eye.
The Being that is in the heart is made of mind, which
is of the nature of light, and yet it is as small as a
grain of rice or barley. And yet this one is the ruler
of everything and it is the lord which governs all the
universe and whatever is in it.

WHEN the cosmic powers were created they fell
headlong into the great restless ocean and were

troubled by hunger and thirst. They said to the Soul: Find a dwelling-place for us, where we may rest and eat food. He brought a bull to them, and they said: This is not enough for us. He brought a horse to them, and they said: This is not enough for us. He brought a man to them, and they said: Oh, well done. For a man is well done. The Soul told them: Enter your respective dwelling-places. So fire became speech and entered the mouth. Wind became breath and entered the nose. The sun became sight and entered the eyes. The regions of heaven became hearing and entered the ears. Plants and trees became hairs and entered the skin. The moon became mind and entered the heart. Then hunger and thirst said to the Soul: Find a dwelling-place for us as well. He replied: I will give you a place among these cosmic powers and make you share with them. Therefore whenever a sacrifice is made to any cosmic power, hunger and thirst partake of it.

* LIX *

THERE were five great householders who were experts in the scriptures and when they met together they considered the questions: What is the Soul? What is Being? They agreed that it was the sage Uddalaka who had studied the Universal Soul and so they went to him with their questions. But Uddalaka was afraid that he might not be able to answer everything and he directed them to another sage. He said: Gentlemen, Ashva-pati has made a special study of this Universal Soul, let us go to him. When they came to Ashva-pati he was performing a sacrifice, so the following

56

morning they came to him with fuel in their hands as
students and posed their questions. Ashva-pati asked
the first householder: Whom do you revere as the Soul?
He replied: The sky, your majesty. The sage said: The
sky which you revere is indeed the Universal Soul, and
that is why there is plenty of food in your family. But
this is only the head of the Soul. Ashva-pati asked the
second householder: Whom do you revere as the Soul?
He replied: The sun, your majesty. The sage said:
The sun which you revere is indeed the Universal
Soul and that is why there is prosperity in your family.
But this is only the eye of the Soul. In like manner
he inquired of the others, who declared that they
worshipped the wind, space, water and earth. Ashva-
pati concluded: You only know this Universal Soul
as something separate, in different regions. But
whosoever reveres the Universal Soul as without
limit, understands all worlds, all beings and all
selves.

* LX *

THERE WAS a young man named Shveta-ketu, son of
the sage Uddalaka. One day he went to an assembly
of rulers and one of them asked him: Young man, has
your father taught you? He replied: Yes, indeed, sir.
Do you know where creatures go when they die? No,
sir. Do you know how they come back again? No, sir.
Do you know the parting of the two ways that lead to
the gods and the ancestors? No, sir. Do you know why
the world beyond is not full up? No, sir. How can you
say that you have been educated? Indeed how can

57

anyone say he is educated who does not know these
things?

★ LXI ★

SHVETA-KETU returned home in distress and com-
plained to his father: You said you had educated me,
without having instructed me. A fellow of the ruling
class asked me several questions and I could not answer
one of them. When Uddalaka heard the questions he
said: I also do not know one of these, for if I had done
would I not have taught you? Uddalaka went to the
assembly-hall and was received with due respect. The
chief prince said to him: Honourable Uddalaka, you
may have any request for wealth. He replied: Wealth
belongs to you, my lord. Please explain what you
said to my son. The prince was troubled and told him
to wait a while. Then he said: This knowledge was
never given to priests before you, but it belonged to the
ruling class, which is why they are rulers. Listen to me.

★ LXII ★

THE PRINCE, Pravahana, instructed the sage Uddalaka
in the journeys of souls after death. He said: Those who
have knowledge, and those who worship in the forest
with austerity, merge into the cremation flame, into
the day, into the bright moon and into the summer
sun. There a supernatural person leads them to the
Supreme Being. That is the way of the gods and there
is no return for them. Those who practise sacrifices in
the village, with works and almsgiving, merge into
the cremation smoke, into the night, into the dark

58

half of the moon and into the winter sun. They enter
the worlds of the ancestors and stay there as long as
there is a remainder from their good deeds. Then they
come back by the same way: into space, wind, smoke,
mist, cloud and rain. They are born on earth as herbs,
plants and trees. It is difficult to get out of that, but
if someone eats them as food and emits them as semen,
they can enter another womb. Those whose conduct
on earth has been pleasant will enter pleasant wombs of
women of priestly or princely or merchant classes. But
those whose conduct has been foul will enter foul
wombs, those of a bitch or a sow or an outcast
woman. That is why the world beyond is not full
up. So one should guard oneself. He who knows this
becomes pure and clean, and attains to a pure world.

⋆ LXIII ⋆

SHVETA-KETU was sent by his father Uddalaka to assist
the priest Chitra in sacrifice. When he arrived Chitra
asked the youth: Does reincarnation come to an end?
Or are there several ways on which one should go?
He replied: I do not know. I must ask my teacher.
He went and told his father the questions and asked
how he should answer. Uddalaka said: I myself do not
know the answer. Let us go and learn from him. Fuel
in hand he went to Chitra and said: Let me be your
pupil. Chitra answered: You deserve to receive this
knowledge since you are not proud. I will teach you.
When men die they rise up to the moon, which is the
door of the heavenly world. If they give the right
reply they go further, but if not they return to earth

in rain. They are born again according to their deeds and according to their knowledge.

CHITRA further told Uddalaka: A soul that passes through the heavenly door arrives at the worlds of the gods. Then five hundred nymphs deck him with robes, garlands and perfumes, and with the knowledge of Being and he proceeds to Being. He comes to an ancient lake and an ageless river, and crosses them with his mind. He casts off his good and evil deeds, which descend to his relatives, his good deeds going to his good relatives and his bad deeds to the bad. The soul arrives at an 'unconquered' palace, an 'extensive' hall and a 'far-shining' throne. There sits the Supreme Being, who asks him: Who are you? He replies: I am what you are. Who am I? The Real. What is the Real? It comprises the universe. You are all the universe.

THE SAGE UDDALAKA said to his son Shveta-ketu: It is time for you to become a student of sacred knowledge, for in our family nobody should be a hanger-on of our class and remain uneducated. So Shveta-ketu became a student at the age of twelve, learned all the scriptures, and returned home at the age of twenty-four, proud of his learning, conceited and obstinate. His father said to him: My dear boy, since you are proud of your learning, conceited and obstinate, did you ask for that teaching by which the unheard becomes heard, the unthought becomes thought, and the unknown becomes known? He replied: What kind of teaching is that, sir? Uddalaka answered: It is this—from one lump of earth everything made of earth can be understood, for the variations are just names and the reality is simply 'earth'. From one copper ornament everything made of copper can be understood, for the variations are just names and the reality is simply 'copper'. From one pair of scissors everything made of iron can be understood, for the variations are just names and the reality is simply 'iron'. Shveta-ketu said: I am sure my revered teachers did not know that, for if they had would they not have told me? But will you please explain this to me? His father said: Very well, my dear.

★ LXVI ★

UDDALAKA instructed Shveta-ketu in the knowledge of the primal unity and the development of the elements. He said: In the beginning, my dear, this universe was simply Being—only one, without a second. It is true that some people say that in the beginning this universe was simply Non-being—only one, without a second. And that Being was produced from Non-being. But how could that be so, my dear? How could Being come out of Non-being? No, on the contrary, this universe was simply Being alone in the beginning —only one, without a second. It considered: Let me be many. Let me procreate. It emitted heat, which emitted water, which emitted food. That Being entered into these three powers with the living Soul of each, and made them distinct in name and form.

61

UDDALAKA taught Shveta-ketu of the nature of sleep and death. He said: You should understand, my dear, the nature of sleep. When a man is sleeping, as it is called, he has reached Being and gone to his own. As a bird tied to a string flies around trying to find a place of rest and then settles down on the very string that holds it captive, so the mind flies around in all directions but finding no rest anywhere else it rests in the Breath of Life. All creatures here have Being as their resting-place, Being as their foundation, Being as their home. When a man is dying his voice is absorbed into his mind, his mind into breath, his breath into heat, his heat into the highest substance. That subtle essence is the Soul of the whole universe. That is Reality. That is the Soul. *You* are That.

UDDALAKA taught Shveta-ketu in a series of parables to illustrate the oneness behind the many appearances, the universal Soul which unites all things. He said: Bees make honey by collecting the juices from different trees and reducing them to unity. Yet those juices cannot distinguish that they are the juice of this tree or that. So, my dear, all creatures here when they merge into Being, do not know that they were individuals when they merged into Being. Whatever they are in this world, tiger or lion, wolf or boar, worm or moth, gnat or fly, they become that Being. That subtle essence is the Soul of the whole universe. That is Reality. That is the Soul. *You* are That.

Shveta-ketu said to his father: Please tell me more, sir. Uddalaka replied: Very well, my dear. The eastern rivers flow to the east and the western flow to the west. They go from sea to sea and become the sea. But when they arrive there they do not know that they were this one or that one. So, my dear, all creatures here when they merge into Being, do not know that they were individuals when they merged into Being. Whatever they are in this world, tiger or lion, wolf or boar, worm or moth, gnat or fly, they become that Being. That subtle essence is the Soul of the whole universe. That is Reality. That is the Soul. *You* are That.

Uddalaka commanded Shveta-ketu: Bring me a fig from that tree. He replied: Here it is, sir. Split it open. I have split it, sir. What do you see in it? These tiny seeds, sir. Split one of them open, please. I have split it, sir. What do you see in it? Nothing, sir. Yet, my dear boy, from a subtle essence which one cannot see, this great fig tree has grown. Have faith, my dear, for that subtle essence is the Soul of the whole universe. That is Reality. That is the Soul. *You* are That.

Uddalaka commanded Shveta-ketu again: Put this salt in water and come back to me in the morning. He did so and the next day his father said: Please bring me the salt which you put in water last evening. The young man felt for it but could not find it, since it had dissolved. Uddalaka said: Please sip the water at this side, what does it taste like? Salty. Sip it in the middle, what is it like? Salty. Sip it from the other side, what is it like? Salty. Throw it away and come to me. He did so, and the salt reappeared by evaporation. Then Uddalaka said: My dear boy, you could not perceive Being here, but in fact it is here. That subtle essence is the Soul of the whole universe. That is Reality. That is the Soul. *You* are That.

⋆ LXXII ⋆

A YOUNG MAN named Narada went to the sage Sanatkumara and besought him: Please teach me, sir. He replied: Tell me what you know and I will develop it further. Narada said: I know the scriptures, the ancient traditions, grammar, mathematics, divination, chronology, logic, politics, government, astronomy, medicine and the fine arts. I know all this but I do not understand the Soul. I have heard from other teachers that he who knows the Soul overcomes sorrow. I am sorrowful, so please help me to overcome sorrow. Sanatkumara said: What you have studied are mere names, in the scriptures, grammar, politics and the rest. These are mere names. Narada asked: Is there anything more than the name? The sage answered: Certainly there is something more than the name. He said: Please tell me what it is.

⋆ LXXIII ⋆

SANATKUMARA said: Speech is more than the name. For speech makes the scriptures, logic, and the rest known.

Narada asked: But is there something more than speech? The sage replied: Certainly there is something more than speech. Please tell me what it is. Mind is more than speech, for as a closed hand grasps two acorns or berries or dice, so mind grasps both speech and name, words and works. Is there anything more than mind? Certainly there is something more than mind. Please tell me what it is. Then Sanatkumara enumerated the different elements: will, thought, meditation, understanding, strength, food, water, heat, space, memory, hope and the breath of life. In each instance Narada asked: Is there more than these? Finally the sage said: There is the Soul. For all these elements arise from the Soul. The Soul is below. The Soul is above. The Soul is to the west. The Soul is to the east. The Soul is to the north. The Soul is to the south. Truly the Soul is the whole universe.

⋆ LXXIV ⋆

ONE DAY the Lord of Creatures spoke in the presence of gods and demons: One should search out and try to understand the Soul—that which is untouched by evil, old age, death, sorrow, hunger and thirst. One who understands the Soul obtains all states and desires. That is Reality. Indra among the gods, and Virochana among the demons, resolved to search out that Soul which would lead to all states and desires. They came to the Lord of Creatures with fuel in their hands as pupils and for thirty-two years they lived as students of sacred knowledge. At the end of that time the Lord asked them: What do you want by living here so long?

They replied: That Soul which is untouched by evil, old age, death, sorrow, hunger and thirst, and grants all states and desires. The Lord said: The Person which is seen in the eye is that Soul about which I spoke, the immortal and fearless. They said: But what about the one that can be seen in water or a mirror? What Person is that? He answered: Look at yourselves in a bowl of water and ask me about it. They did so and said: We see a Self just like our own, even to the hairs and finger-nails. The Lord said: That is the Soul, immortal and fearless. That is Being. They went away and Virochana told the demons: You must look after your own Self and make yourself happy on earth to gain all the worlds, here and hereafter. That is the belief of demons to this day. By adorning the body alone they think they will gain this world and the next.

★ LXXV ★

INDRA, however, was not satisfied, and before he reached the gods he saw a difficulty. He returned to the Lord of Creatures, fuel in hand as a student. The Lord said: Why have you come back, since you went away with Virochana in peace? Indra replied: The bodily self may be well dressed and adorned, but if the body is blind or lame or maimed then the self will be also, and it perishes with the body. There is nothing good here. The Lord said: That is true. But live with me for thirty-two years and I will explain it further. After that time the Lord said: It is the Self that wanders about happily in dreams that is immortal and fearless. That is Being.

INDRA went away serenely but before reaching the gods
he saw a difficulty. He returned to the Lord of
Creatures, fuel in hand. The Lord asked: Why have
you come back, since you went away in peace? Indra
replied: If the self in dreams is not blind when the
body is blind, if it is not lame when the body is lame,
or does not suffer with the body's ailments, yet it does
have the feeling of suffering. In sleep it seems to be
killed, or naked, or sorrowing, and it even weeps.
There is nothing good here. The Lord said: That is true.
But live with me for thirty-two more years and I will
explain it further. After that time the Lord said: When
one is fast asleep, calm and composed in dreamless
sleep, that is the Self that is immortal and fearless. That
is Being.

INDRA went away serenely but before reaching the
gods he saw a further difficulty. He returned to the
Lord of Creatures, fuel in hand. The Lord asked: Why
have you come back, since you went away in peace?
Indra replied: This Self in dreamless sleep has no
knowledge of himself, he does not think 'I am this'.
He knows nothing of the world and might as well be
annihilated. There is nothing good here. The Lord
said: That is true. But live with me for five more years
and I will explain it further. So Indra had lived with
the Lord of Creatures for a hundred and one years as a
student of sacred knowledge. Then the Lord said:
The body is mortal and is held by death, but it is the

dwelling of the immortal and bodiless Soul. As long as it is in the body it is held by pleasure and pain, but when it is freed from the body these cannot touch it. It is this Soul which thinks and sees and rejoices. All beings revere this Soul, and one who understands the Soul obtains all states and desires.

* LXXVIII *

THERE WAS a great sage named Kaushitaki who used to worship the rising sun. He was the first about whom it is recorded that he wore the sacred thread of the twice-born over the left shoulder. Having put on the sacred thread he sipped water three times, sprinkled the water-vessel three times, and invoked the sun, saying: You are the deliverer. Deliver me from evil. In like manner he worshipped the sun at midday, saying: You are the deliverer. Deliver me from evil. In like manner at sunset he worshipped the sun, saying: You are the deliverer. Deliver me from evil. Whatever wrong he committed by day or night, it was taken away. So he who understands this worships the sun in the same way, and whatever evil he commits by day or night it is taken away.

* LXXIX *

PRATARDANA was a prince who had shown great courage in battle, and after death he arrived at the much-desired heaven of the god Indra. Indra said to him: Pratardana, choose a boon. He replied: Please choose yourself the gift which will bring the most good to mankind. But Indra said: A superior does not choose

68

for an inferior. Choose it yourself. Pratardana retorted:
In that case it would not be a boon. Then Indra said:
That which would bring the most good to mankind is
to understand me. I am the Breath of Life and the
intelligent Self. So reverence me as life and immortality. Life is breath and breath is life. Therefore the
Breath of Life is immortality. There is life as long as the
Breath of Life remains in the body. And by the Breath
of Life one obtains immortality in the next world,
with intelligence and true understanding. Whoever
reverences me as life and immortality wins a full span
of days in this world, and immortality and indestructi-
bility in heaven.

* LXXX *

THE SUPREME BEING gave victory to the gods and they
rejoiced in it, but they thought it had come about by
their own power. The Supreme Being knew this
and appeared to the gods but they did not recognize
him. They said: What is this strange creature? They
told the Fire: All-knowing one, find out what this
strange creature is. The Fire ran towards that Being
and it asked him: Who are you? He replied: I am
Fire, the All-knowing. What power have you?
I can burn up anything on earth. It put a straw in front
of him and said: Burn that. The Fire ran upon it with
all its might but could not burn the straw. It went back
to the gods and told them: I could not find out about
this, what this strange creature is.

★ LXXXI ★

THE GODS said to the Wind: Find out what this strange creature is. The Wind ran towards that Being and it asked him: Who are you? He replied: I am Wind, the one within the fire-sticks. What power have you? I can blow away anything on earth. It put a straw in front of him and said: Blow that. The Wind ran upon it with all its might but could not move the straw. It went back to the gods and told them: I could not find out about this, what this strange creature is.

★ LXXXII ★

THE GODS said to Indra: Bountiful one, find out what this strange creature is. Indra ran towards that Being but it had disappeared. But in that place Indra met a beautiful woman, Uma, the daughter of the snowy Himalaya mountains. He asked her: What is this strange creature? She replied: It is Brahman, the Supreme Being. You have been rejoicing in his victory. So Indra knew that it was the Supreme Being and therefore Indra is above all other gods because he was the first to know the Supreme Being.

★ LXXXIII ★

THE SAGE UDDALAKA was giving away all his possessions in order to gain merit. He had a son named Nachiketas and although he was only a boy he was filled with faith. As cows were brought up as fees for the sacrifice he thought to himself: Those cows are barren, their milk has gone, they had no water to drink or grass to eat. He who gives such cows will

surely go to unhappy worlds. Nachiketas said to his
father: Papa, why not offer *me*? He asked him a second
time: Papa, why not offer *me*? He asked him a third
time: Papa, why not offer *me*? His father was angry
and said: Oh, go to Hades! I will offer you to
Death!

* LXXXIV *

NACHIKETAS went away to the world beyond, thinking: I am going as the first of many, I am going as the
intermediary of many, what will Death do with me if
I belong to him? I look backwards to see how men
went of old, and forwards to see how others will go.
Man ripens like corn and like corn he is born again.
Nachiketas belonged to a priestly family and anticipa-
ted the hospitality due to priests. In the other world,
however, Death was absent for three days and on his
return he found that Nachiketas had remained without
food. Death said: You are a priest and deserve reverence, but you have dwelt in my house for three days
without eating. I salute you now and may welfare be
mine. In recompense for this neglect, please make
three wishes.

* LXXXV *

NACHIKETAS chose as his first wish that his father might
be appeased and his anger quelled. He said: O Death,
let Uddalaka be well disposed and free from anger, so
that if I am released from you he may receive me back
with kindness. I choose this as my first wish. Death
replied: Uddalaka will be kind to you and I shall

71

release you. Your father will sleep quietly at night and be free from passion, when he sees you released from the jaws of Death.

NACHIKETAS chose as his second wish the knowledge of the sacrificial fire that leads men to heaven. He said: There is no fear in heaven, and you yourself are not there. No one in heaven fears old age or hunger or thirst or sorrow, and happiness is there. You, O Death, understand the heavenly fire, and the world where there is immortality. Explain this to me since I have faith, and I choose this as my second wish. Death replied: I will tell you about the heavenly fire, for it is hidden in secret places and will bring you to the endless world. Moreover, I will give you a further wish, in that henceforth this ritual will be known by your own name, and be called the Nachiketas-fire. By knowing this sacred word and the divine Being, one goes to peace for ever.

NACHIKETAS chose as his third wish the knowledge of the destiny of the soul after death. He said: When a man dies there are doubts about his fate. Some say that he exists, others that he does not. I want to settle my doubts. This is my third wish. Death replied: The very gods have doubted this since ancient times. It is a difficult and subtle matter. Choose another wish, Nachiketas, excuse me on this one and do not insist. He answered: Maybe the gods have had doubts about this and it is not easy to understand. But who else beside you, O Death, could tell me the answer, and what other wish could be like this? Death said: I will grant you any other wish. Choose sons and grandsons living a hundred years; choose cattle and elephants, gold and horses; choose great property and as many years as you like; choose lovely women, with musical instruments such as cannot be obtained by men. But ask me no more about dying. Nachiketas insisted: These are ephemeral things, for mortal powers wear away and a whole life is very short. Man cannot be satisfied with wealth and what use are riches when we have seen Death? This thing that men have doubts about, tell me that. What is there in the great passing-on?

* LXXXVIII *

DEATH commended Nachiketas for steadily rejecting desires, possessions and praise. He said: A wise man puts joy and sorrow behind him, and engages in the Yoga exercise which concerns the soul. Let him think about that God who is hard to see, primeval, dwelling in the depths, set in the secret places of the heart. This is the word which all the scriptures repeat, which all austerities proclaim, for love of which men study sacred knowledge, and I will tell you that word briefly in these verses:

> The soul never dies and never born is he,
> came not into being and never comes to be,
> primeval, in the body's death unslain,
> unborn, eternal, everlastingly.

Both he who thinks this soul can kill
and he who thinks that it is killed
have neither truly understood,
it does not kill and is never killed.

★ LXXXIX ★

DEATH taught Nachiketas further about the nature of
the indestructible soul. He said: The Soul that is in the
heart of creatures is smaller than the small, and greater
than the great. One who is free from desire beholds it
and is released from sorrow. By the grace of the
Creator he beholds the greatness of the Soul. This Soul
is not to be obtained by teaching, nor by intellect nor
learning. He is gained only by the one whom he
chooses, and to that man the Soul reveals its own true
nature. But one who has not ceased from doing
wrong, who has no peace or concentration, whose
mind is restless, cannot obtain him however clever he
may be.

★ XC ★

DEATH said: The Soul is a rider in a chariot. The body
is the car, the intellect is the driver, the mind is the
reins. The senses are the horses, and their objects are
the road, while the Soul experiences everything
combined with the senses and the mind. He whose
mind is undisciplined, who has no intelligence,
has uncontrolled senses like the unruly horses of a
charioteer. But he who is intelligent, whose mind is
disciplined, keeps his senses under control like the
trained horses of a good charioteer. He who is not

intelligent, who is thoughtless and impure, does not reach the goal but returns in the round of reincarnation. But he who is intelligent, who is thoughtful and pure, attains the goal and is not born again on earth. If his charioteer is wisdom, and his mind controls the reins, he reaches the end of his journey and the highest place of God.

★ XCI ★

THIS TALE of Nachiketas, with the ancient teaching given by Death, brings joy and bliss to those who hear and declare it. This supreme mystery fits one for immortality.

> The objects of sense are higher than sense,
> reason is higher than objects of sense,
> higher than reason is the mind,
> the Great Soul is higher than the mind.

> Beyond the Great Soul is the Unmanifest
> and Spirit beyond the Unmanifest,
> beyond the Spirit is nothing at all
> for that is the Way and the highest Goal.

★ XCII ★

DEATH further instructed Nachiketas in the nature of the soul and its reincarnation or liberation. The eleven gates of the body are either eleven senses or eleven openings through which the soul leaves the body. By ruling over the city with eleven gates, the soul that is unborn and of unwavering intelligence has no sorrow, and when he is freed from the body he is free indeed.

75

That is the truth. Come, I will explain the mystery of the eternal Being, and what happens to the soul after death. Some souls go into a womb and receive another body. Others go into a lifeless state. Everything happens according to their actions and their knowledge. But the Spirit that is awake among the sleepers, who considers all desires, he is the pure, he is Being. That is the Immortal on which all the worlds rest and no one goes beyond it. That is the truth.

⋆ XCIII ⋆

DEATH spoke of the cosmic tree which is rooted in Being, the cosmic Soul. This is the eternal Fig-tree, whose root is above and whose branches are below. That root is the Pure, that is Being, that is Immortal. All the worlds are established in it and no one can pass beyond it. That is the truth. His form is not visible, for no one perceives him with the eye. He is conceived by the heart, the thought and the mind. Those who know this become immortal.

⋆ XCIV ⋆

DEATH spoke briefly of Yoga discipline; yoking the senses, and yoking the soul to God. Yoga is said to be the firm control of the senses, by which one becomes undisturbed. Yoga is the effort and the goal. The Soul cannot be grasped by speech or thought or sight. How then can it be understood except by saying: He is? When all desires that lurk in the heart are expelled, then a mortal becomes immortal, then he reaches Being. When all the knots of the heart are cut, then a mortal becomes immortal. That is the end of my teaching.

WHEN NACHIKETAS had received this knowledge declared by Death, and all the method of Yoga, he attained to that Being. He became free from passion and free from death. And so may anyone else who has this knowledge of the Soul. The Inner Soul is a spirit the size of a thumb, which always dwells in the heart of creatures. One should draw him out from the body firmly, as an arrow is drawn out of a sheath. One should know him as the Pure and Immortal. May this wisdom which Nachiketas received bring help to us all. May it inspire our efforts and bring us glory. May we live without disputes. OM. Peace—peace—peace.

THERE WAS a wise man called Kapeya who was eating with a friend, and while they were being served a student of sacred knowledge begged food from them, but they gave him nothing. So the student propounded this riddle: Who is the one God, the world-protector, who has swallowed up four mighty beings? He abides in different forms but mortals do not perceive him. You have offered no food to the one to whom it belongs, Kapeya. Kapeya thought about this and answered: It is the Soul of gods, creator of beings, whose golden teeth devour everything and who is truly wise. His power is great, because he devours what is not food, and he is not eaten himself. O student of sacred knowledge, we reverence the universal Soul. Kapeya called his servants and told them to give the student food. Indeed food is primal matter and through it the whole world becomes seen. Whoever knows this understands the whole universe.

A YOUNG MAN Bhrigu went to his father, the wise Varuna, and asked him: Sir, explain Being to me. Varuna replied: It is that from which all creatures are born, by which they live, and into which they enter when they die. That is Being. Bhrigu said: Explain Being further, sir. He replied: You must try to understand Being by self-denial, for Being is austerity. So Bhrigu performed ascetic practices and he came to understand that Being is food, and breath, and mind, and understanding, and bliss. But especially food. For all beings are born from food, they live by food, and when they die they enter into food. He cried: Wonderful! Wonderful! Wonderful! I am food! I am food! I am food! I am an eater of food. I am a maker of verses. I am the firstborn in the world. I have overcome the world.

THE SAGE VAMADEVA asked: Who is the one that we should worship? The answer came: It is the Soul. He said: Which Soul is that? The answer came: It is the one by whom one sees, and hears, and smells, and speaks and distinguishes. He is heart and mind, consciousness and perception, discrimination and intelligence, wisdom and insight, steadfastness and thought, thoughtfulness and impulse, memory and conception, will and life, desire and power. All these are names of wisdom. He is Being: the gods, the elements, all life and all creatures, whatever moves or is still. All this is guided by wisdom and based on wisdom. The world is guided by wisdom and its basis is wisdom. Being is wisdom. Vamadeva rose up on high from this world by that intelligent Soul, obtained the joys of heaven, and became immortal, Yes, he became that.

* XCIX *

ANOTHER SAGE said: All the universe is pervaded by the Lord, whatever moving things there are in the moving world. Renounce it, that you may enjoy it. Do not covet the wealth of anyone.

* C *

THERE WAS a great householder named Shaunaka who approached the sage Angiras in the formal way. Angiras had received both the higher and the lower wisdom from older teachers, who traced a long succession back to the first of the gods. He had imparted the knowledge of Being, as the basis of all wisdom. Shaunaka asked: What should I know, sir, by which I might understand the whole universe? Angiras replied: Those who are experts in Being say that there are two kinds of wisdom, a higher and a lower. The lower is concerned with ritual texts and chants. The higher brings understanding of the

Imperishable Being. He continued: That which is invisible and intangible, without family or class, without eye or ear, hands or feet, eternal, pervading, penetrating, subtle—that is the Imperishable Being which wise men have perceived to be the origin of all things. As a spider spins out and draws in again its threads, as plants grow from the ground, and as hair grows on the head and body of a living man, so everything here arises from the Imperishable Being.

★ CI ★

ANGIRAS said: Those who have faith, and lead an ascetic life in the forest, who are wise and peaceful and live on gifts, when they die will pass without trouble through the doorway of the sun to where the immortal Being dwells, the unchanging Soul. One who seeks this knowledge should go, fuel in hand, to a spiritual teacher who knows the scriptures and is established in that Being. One who comes respectfully, with mind serene and peaceful, will be taught by such a wise teacher the knowledge of that one by which he knows the Imperishable Being and the Truth.

★ CII ★

ANGIRAS said:

The Supreme Being is divine and formless,
he is within and without,
he is not breath or mind,
he is pure and higher than the Imperishable itself.

80

Breath is produced from him,
the mind and all the senses,
space, wind, light and water,
and earth which supports everything.

His head is fire,
sun and moon are his eyes,
his ears are the regions of space,
his voice is the revealed scripture,
his breath is wind,
his heart is the whole world,
and from his feet came the earth.
Indeed he is the Inner Soul of all beings.

★ CIII ★

ANGIRAS spoke this parable: Two birds who are close
companions cling to the same tree. One of them eats
the sweet fruit, but the other looks on and eats
nothing. On such a tree a man sits plunged in sorrow
and perplexity because of his lack of power but when
he sees the other, the Lord in his greatness, then he is
content and freed from grief. When a seer perceives
the brilliant Creator, the Lord, the Spirit, the Source of
Being, then he understands. He casts away good and
evil, is freed from stains, and attains to the highest unity
with him.

★ CIV ★

THIS IS THE TRUTH which the sage Angiras declared in
olden days: As rivers flow down into the sea and lose
their names and forms, so the man who knows the
truth is freed from name and form and goes to the

divine Being who is higher than the highest. Truly whoever knows that Supreme Being really becomes Being. He passes beyond sorrow and sin, and freed from the knots of the heart he becomes immortal. One may declare this knowledge of Being to those who worship, know the scriptures, have faith, and offer themselves to the one Seer. But those who have not dedicated themselves should not study it.

Salutation to the greatest sages.
Salutation to the greatest sages.

⋆ CV ⋆

THERE WERE six men who were devoted to the universal Being, intent on that Being, and seeking for the Supreme Being. They came to the sage Pippalada, with fuel in their hands as pupils, thinking that he if anyone would solve their problems. Pippalada said to them: If you spend a year with me in ascetic practices, chastity and faith, then ask what you will and if I can I will tell you the answer. After that time Kabandhin approached him and asked: Sir, where did all these creatures come from? Pippalada replied: It was the Lord of Creatures who wanted to produce offspring. He practised austerity and by its power he produced a pair, matter and spirit, knowing that these two would reproduce themselves in many different creatures.

⋆ CVI ⋆

THEN BHARGAVA asked the sage: How many powers support a creature? Which give it light, and which

82

is the greatest of them? Pippalada replied: Space is one of these powers, and others are wind, fire, water and earth. Then there are speech, mind, sight and hearing; all these give light and sustain creatures. The greatest of these is the Breath of Life, for it divides itself and sustains creatures. As all the bees rise up when the queen bee rises, and all settle down again when she settles down, so speech, mind, sight and hearing follow the Breath of Life and are content to give it praise. O Lord of Creatures, you move in the womb and you yourself are born again. To you, O Breath of Life, all creatures bring their gifts, for you dwell in living beings. All the universe, even up to the third heaven, is controlled by the Breath of Life. Protect us as a mother cares for her son, and grant us prosperity and wisdom.

* CVII *

KAUSALYA asked Pippalada: Where does the Breath of Life come from? How does it enter the body? How does it distribute and fix itself there? How does it go away again? How is it related to the outside world? How is it related to the Soul? The sage replied: You ask too many questions, but I think you are a serious scholar so I will tell you. He continued: The Breath of Life comes from the Soul, and it enters the body by the action of the mind from a previous existence, as a shadow follows a man. Then the Breath of Life gives the other powers their tasks, as a master commands his overseers to govern different villages. The lesser breaths are fixed in the various organs and the Soul is in the heart with its thousands of arteries and veins.

When the breath departs it rises up through one of these channels either to a good world resulting from good deeds, or to an evil world resulting from evil deeds. In the outer world the sun is the Breath of Life and it is related to the Breath of Life in the eye. The Breath of Life together with the Soul leads a man on to the next world which his mind has fashioned.

* CVIII *

GARGYA asked: Sir, what are those things which sleep in a man? What are those that stay awake? Which is the power that sees dreams? Which one enjoys happiness? And what are they all based upon? Pippalada replied: When the sun is setting all its rays become one in a bright circle, and when it rises they shoot out again. So in sleep everything in the body becomes one in the highest power, which is the mind. In that state man does not smell, taste, touch, speak, grasp, enjoy sex, excrete or move around. Men say that he is asleep. But in this city of the body the fires of the Breath of Life remain awake, as the sacrificial fires are kept alight. It is the mind which has great experiences in sleep, remembering what it has seen or heard or felt in different times and places. It sees also what it has not seen or heard or felt, for it sees everything. But in deep sleep it has no dreams and happiness comes. As birds settle on a tree to make their nests, so, my friend, everything here is based upon the Supreme Soul. The one who sees, touches, hears, smells, tastes, thinks, perceives and acts, the conscious self, he comes to rest in the Supreme Imperishable Soul.

84

SATYAKAMA asked: Sir, if a man were to meditate on the mystical syllable OM to the end of his life, what state of being would he gain by that? Pippalada replied: The syllable OM is both the higher and the lower knowledge, and it can lead a man to either. By the lower knowledge, with austerity and chastity and faith, one may attain spiritual growth. Such a man gains a heavenly world after death but he will return to earth again. By the higher knowledge, meditating on the Supreme Being, with the fullness of OM, one is united with the glory of the sun. As a snake is freed from its old skin, so this man is freed from evil. He beholds that Being which is higher than the highest and yet dwells in the body. Eventually the wise man attains to the Supreme which is peaceful, ageless, immortal and fearless.

SUKESHA said: Sir, a prince came to me and inquired if I knew about the person of sixteen parts, and I had to confess that I did not know him, for it is not right to tell lies. So the prince got back into his chariot in silence and drove away. Now I ask you, sir, where is that person? Pippalada replied, My friend, here in your own body is that person from whom they say sixteen parts arise. The Supreme Being emanated the Breath of Life, and from it came sixteen elements in names and forms. As rivers when they flow into the sea disappear in name and form, and it is simply called 'the sea', even so the sixteen parts of a person when they reach

the Supreme Being disappear in name and form and
are simply called 'Being'. That one has no parts and is
immortal. Then Pippalada concluded his discussions
by saying: This, truly, is what I know about that
Supreme Being. There is nothing higher than That.
The six students praised him and said: Indeed you are
our father, for you have taken us across the river of
ignorance to the shore of truth.

Salutation to the greatest sages.
Salutation to the greatest sages.

★ CXI ★

THERE WERE ascetics living in the forest called
Valakhilyas, small in size but of considerable numbers.
They were noted for chastity, had freed themselves
from evil and shone in glory. They asked the Lord of
Creatures: Sir, the body is like a cart without intelligence, but what superior being is it that directs a cart
so that it appears to be intelligent? In short, who is its
driver? He replied: It is that one who seems to stand
aloof, like those who though surrounded by the
faculties of nature abstain from them. He is pure, clean,
void, serene; not breath, not self, infinite, unchange-
able, stable, eternal, unborn and independent. He
stands in his own glory and directs the body so that it
seems to be intelligent. In short, that is its driver. They
asked: If this being is indifferent, how can it make the
body appear to be intelligent? How can it be its driver?
The Lord answered: That subtle, intangible, invisible
one who is known as the Spirit inspires the body with

only a fragment of himself. There is no previous awareness of him in the body beforehand, just as a sleeper awakes without having had any previous awareness of waking. He moves the body by his intelligence, so that it seems to be intelligent itself, but he is the driver. He said further: Poets say that this Soul wanders from body to body on earth, but it is untouched by the good and evil results of actions. He is permanent but does not act, because he is unmanifest, subtle, invisible, intangible and pure. He enjoys good works and is concealed by the veil of the faculties of nature, but he remains ever the same and eternally stable.

★ CXII ★

THE VALAKHILYA ascetics asked the Lord of Creatures: Sir, if this Spirit is so great, it would seem that there is another different one, also called the Soul, which is affected by the good and evil results of actions. This one enters good and evil wombs, so that it rises and falls in the round of existence. The Lord replied: There is indeed another soul which is called the Individual or Elemental Soul. This is the one which is affected by the good and evil results of actions, so that it enters good and evil wombs and rises and falls in the round of existence. This Elemental Soul is overcome by the faculties of nature and becomes so confused that it does not perceive the Blessed Lord who dwells within individual souls. It is carried along and infected by the faculties of nature, becoming unstable, fickle, bewildered, distracted and full of desires. It thinks itself to be a separate person and imagines 'I am this, this is mine', and so it is bound by itself like a bird caught in a net. This is why the Elemental Soul is filled with passions, and it takes on many different forms. Indeed it assumes many different forms.

★ CXIII ★

THE HOLY VALAKHILYAS were astonished at these words and they cried out together: Sir, we give you homage. Please teach us more, for you are our refuge and there is no other. In what way can this Elemental Soul achieve union with the Supreme Soul when it leaves the body at death? The Lord of Creatures replied: As the direction of waves in a river cannot be turned back, so actions that have been done cannot be reversed. As the ocean tides cannot be stopped, no more can the approach of death. The Elemental Soul is like a lame man, bound with the chains of his good and evil deeds. It is like a man in prison, bound by someone else. It is like a man in Hades, full of fear. It is like a drunken man, full of delusions. It is like a man possessed by an evil spirit, rushing here and there. It is like a man bitten by a snake, bitten by sensual things. It is like a man in darkness, the darkness of passion. It is like a victim of jugglery, deceived by illusion. It is like a dreamer seeing false appearances. It is like an empty reed, having no core. It is like an actor, wearing a temporary costume. It is like a painted picture, deceiving the mind. For the objects that a man strives after, in sound and touch and sense, are worthless. By clinging to them the Elemental Soul forgets its highest goal.

88

THE LORD OF CREATURES continued: There is an antidote for these temptations of the Elemental Soul. It consists in study of the scriptures and performance of one's own duty. To do one's duty, according to each stage of life, whether as student or householder or forest-dweller, that is the rule. All other rules are like chaff. However, if one is not disciplined there is little progress towards knowledge of the Soul or perfection in actions. Goodness is gained from austerity, and the mind is gained from goodness. The Soul is gained from the mind, and having gained it one does not return to earth after death. When the driver of the chariot, the individual Soul, is freed from all those things which held and filled him, then he attains to full union with the cosmic Soul.

THE VALAKHILYAS said to the Lord of Creatures: Sir, you are the greatest speaker and expounder. What you have said has been kept in our minds. Please answer one more question. Some men meditate upon one god and some upon another, but which is the best? He replied: All these gods are the principal forms of the formless and immortal Supreme Being. A man will enjoy the world of whichever god he follows, for the Supreme Being contains the whole universe. One should meditate on the great forms and praise them, but then one should discard them! With these gods one may rise higher in different worlds.

But when the universe is all dissolved one attains to the
unity of Being, yes of Being indeed.

THE GREAT WHITE SAGE Shveta-shvatara, by the effect
of discipline and by the grace of God, declared the
knowledge of Being in the right way. He spoke to
ascetics in the most advanced stage of life for their
highest purification and to the community of sages he
gave great joy. He put to them questions raised by
students of sacred knowledge:

> What is the cause of everything?
> What is Being?
> Where did we come from?
> By what power do we live?
> On what are we founded?
> Who directs us, in our various states
> of pain and pleasure?
> Tell us this, O you philosophers.
>
> Is it Time that is the cause?
> Or Nature? Or Fate? Or accident?
> Or the elements? Or a male or female being?
> Or is it a combination of all these?
> No, it cannot be so, because of the existence
> of the Soul. And the Soul itself is powerless
> over the cause of pleasure and pain.
>
> Wise men in their meditation
> and in the discipline of Yoga
> have seen the power of God
> concealed in his attributes.

He is the One,
who directs all the causes we spoke about
from Time to the Soul.

⋆ CXVII ⋆

SHVETA-SHVATARA spoke of the knowledge of God:
He is the One who spreads his net and with his
sovereign powers governs all the universe. He is the
only One who abides, while others arise and grow.
Those who know this become immortal. He is the One
who has no colour himself but by his power distributes
many colours in his hidden purposes. All things come
from him and at the end the whole universe dissolves
into him. He is God. May he give us a clear mind. He
is the One who governs every womb, in whom the
universe grows together and then dissolves. He is the
Lord, the adorable God, the giver of blessings. By
discerning him one attains to peace for ever. We know
him as gracious yet very subtle. He is hidden in all
things, like cream in butter. He is the One who
encompasses the universe. By knowing God one is
freed from all bonds.

⋆ CXVIII ⋆

SHVETA-SHVATARA spoke of the cosmic Being beyond
and within the soul:

The cosmic Being has a thousand heads,
a thousand eyes and a thousand feet;
he surrounds the earth on every side
and goes beyond it by the breadth of ten fingers.

He has hands and feet on every side,
eyes, heads and mouths on every side,
he has ears on every side and stands
encompassing everything in the world.

The Soul is hidden in the heart of creatures
smaller than the small and greater than the great.
Without the active will, but by the grace of the Creator
man may see the Lord in his greatness
and become free from sorrow.

⋆ CXIX ⋆

SHVETA-SHVATARA spoke of the immanence of the
divine Being:

You are woman, you are man.
You are the youth and also the maiden.
You are the old man tottering with a staff.
When you are born your face turns in every direction.

You are the dark blue bird,
the green parrot with red eyes.
The lightning is your child,
you are the seasons and the seas.
You had no beginning, but you abide in all things.
From you all creatures were born.

⋆ CXX ⋆

THE WISE Shveta-shvatara gave rules for the practice
of Yoga meditation and discipline: Hold the body still
and upright, draw the mind and senses into the heart,
and so a wise man will cross over the rivers of fear on

the Boat of Being. Restrain the breath and control all movements, breathe quietly through the nose, and hold the mind in check like a chariot harnessed to vicious horses. Meditate in a clean and level place, where there are no stones, gravel or fire. Let it be a quiet spot, sheltered from the wind, not offensive but pleasing to the mind by the presence of water and gentle sounds. There may be apparitions of fog, smoke, sun, fire, wind, flies, lightning, crystals and the moon. But these are preliminary visions which prepare for the fuller manifestation of Being in Yoga. The first stage in the path of Yoga brings light, health and steadiness, with a clear complexion, a pleasant voice and a sweet smell. As a mirror which was coated with dust shines brightly when it has been cleaned, so an embodied being, once he has perceived the nature of the Soul, becomes unified, free from sorrow, and attains his goal. A practitioner of Yoga perceives the true nature of Being by using his soul like a lamp. He comes to know the unborn and stable Being, beyond all nature, and knowing God he is freed from all bonds.

★ CXXI ★

SHVETA-SHVATARA spoke again of nature and God: Some wise men say that Nature was the first cause, and others that it was Time. They are both deluded! For it is by the greatness of God in the world that this wheel of Being was made to revolve. He is the One who for ever encompasses the universe. He is intelligent, creator of Time, possessed of attributes, and omniscient. He commands every action which evolves

93

in the five elements of earth, water, fire, air and space. He does his work and then rests again. The one God spins out threads from himself like a spider, and produced nature out of his own essence. The one God is hidden in everything and pervades everywhere, as the Inner Soul of all beings. He is eternal among eternals, intelligent among intelligences, the One among many who grants all wishes. He is the cause of all, who can be understood both by the theory of wisdom and the practice of Yoga. He is the ruler of matter and spirit, the cause of the round of transmigration, the cause of bondage in our stay here, and the cause of salvation. As men cannot roll up space like a piece of leather, so there is no end of sorrow without the knowledge of God.

★ CXXII ★

THE WISE Shveta-shvatara gave this knowledge by the grace of God and brought his sayings to an end in the presence of ascetics and sages: The supreme mystery of the scriptures has been declared since former times, but it should not be told to a man whose passions are not subdued, or who is not a son or a student of knowledge. To a man of high spirit, who has great love for God and reveres his spiritual teacher as God, all these subjects which have been discussed will shine forth with the clearest light. Yes, they will shine forth if he is of high spirit.